# DON'T SELL. LET THEM BUY.™

## MASTER THE SALES CONVERSATION AND GUIDE YOUR CUSTOMERS TO A SUCCESSFUL OUTCOME ... *EVERY TIME*

**Chiqeeta Jameson**
Award-Winning Sales Expert
Coach and Speaker

DON'T SELL. LET THEM BUY.™

MASTER THE SALES CONVERSATION
AND GUIDE YOUR CUSTOMERS TO A
SUCCESSFUL OUTCOME ... *EVERY TIME*

By Chiqeeta Jameson

Copyright ©2017 Chiqeeta Jameson
All Rights Reserved

The author may be contacted at: **www.ChiqeetaJameson.com** or
Email: **cj@ChiqeetaJameson.com.**

Cover Design by Lisa Bollow
Photography by Starla Fortunato

Published in the United States of America
Printed by CreateSpace

First Edition

ISBN - 13: 978-1976348419  (Europe)
ISBN - 10: 1976348412

All rights reserved. No part of this publication may be reproduced, distributed, or transmitted in any form or by any means, including photocopying, recording, or other electronic or mechanical methods, or by any information storage and retrieval system, without the prior written permission of the publisher and author, except in the case of brief quotations embodied in reviews and certain other non-commercial uses permitted by copyright law.

*This book is dedicated...*

*To my parents,
Steve and Dorothy Verban –
for passing their Midwest values onto me,
including the importance of serving others
and that doing the right thing for the right reason
is never wrong.
I miss you every day.*

*To my sister and brother-in-law,
Quita and Dr. George D. Shier –
for being there for me when mom and dad couldn't be
and for their endless, and many ways of, support.
I am so grateful to be your little "Sis."*

*And,
To my husband, gift from God and best friend,
Craig Allen Jameson –
for his quiet steadiness, his ever-present wisdom,
and his unwavering support and belief in me.
It is an honor to be your lifetime partner.
It's also a lot of fun!*

# Table of Contents

**Don't Sell. Let Them Buy, Steps of the Conversation Process Overview** — i

**Introduction** — iii

**Chapter 1** — 1
Does Your Sales Career Make You Happy?

**Chapter 2** — 13
How to Earn the Right to Ask the Customer to Buy from You

**Chapter 3** — 23
How to Prepare Don't Sell. Let Them Buy, Sales Conversations

**Chapter 4** — 61
Overview of the 9-Step Don't Sell. Let Them Buy, Sales Conversation Process

**Chapter 5** — 73
Step 1: Assume the Lead -- How to Set the Stage for the Sales Conversation

**Chapter 6** — 81
Step 2: Ask, Listen, Learn -- How to Engage, Connect, And Understand How to Create Value

**Chapter 7** — 111
Step 3: Summarize -- How to Ensure That You and Your Customers Are On the Same Page

**Chapter 8** — 119
Step 4: Educate -- How to Prove the Value of Your Products and Services

**Chapter 9**    129
Step 5: Recommendation -- How to Present Your
Don't Sell. Let Them Buy, Recommendations

**Chapter 10**    147
Step 6: Answer Concerns -- How to Handle Objections
And Brush-Offs

**Chapter 11**    175
Step 7: Gain Agreement and Finalize -- How to Ask
The Customer to Buy and Finalize the Sales Conversation

**Chapter 12**    191
Step: 8 Follow-Through -- How to Keep Promises
You Make to Your Customers

**Chapter 13**    197
Step 9: Show Gratitude -- How to Create Loyal Fans

**Chapter 14**    209
Final Thoughts from the Author

**Don't Sell. Let Them Buy, Steps of the Conversation**    223
**Process Overview**

**References**    225

**Acknowledgements & Expressions of Gratitude**    227

**About the Author**    235

Don't Sell. Let Them Buy.™

## Steps of the Don't Sell. Let Them Buy™ Sales Conversation Process

Don't Sell. Let Them Buy. ™

## Introduction

You are reading this book for a reason.

Are you looking for answers? Ideas? A kick in the rear-end? Consider it done after reading the following pages. I believe that anyone can learn how to sell. Speaking from 30 years of experience, working for large corporations in telephone and outside sales, it takes commitment, effort, and lots of practice to become a consistent six-figure sales success. I stepped in it, over it, and on top of it, but I finally got it. You will too if you stick with it and believe you can do it.

I finally learned how to sell when I stopped "selling" and began "serving." When you choose to "serve" your customers, you will create elated clients, dedicated fans, and increased productivity.

Speaking of "choice" – a choice is an intentional decision you make when faced with two or more possibilities. All choices have consequences: good, bad, or indifferent. Generally, those who consciously make "choices" take responsibility for their actions; they learn from the consequences of their decisions and choose to live more fulfilling lives. Funny how that works.

## Introduction

And, then, there are mistakes. A mistake is an action with an unintended outcome. For example, your intention may have been to compliment your customer; but, because you were nervous, you accidentally offended them instead. This is embarrassing, but you quickly learn how not to make a repeat performance. Mistakes are necessary for learning to occur. Own this concept. It's true.

In the pages that follow, I will show you how to open your mind to a new way of thinking about your company, your products, and most importantly, your customers.

I will also give you a proven structure that will create a comfortable environment for you and your customers to engage in meaningful conversations, which will result in success. That kind of "success" should always be what is best for your customer.

It took me years of doing all the wrong things, and not enough of the right things before I finally got it. When I made the conscious choice to focus on what is best for my customers, when I made the conscious choice to "serve" my customers, my life became easier, more abundant, and more fulfilling. Yes, I made mistake after mistake but making mistakes is how you learn. And, if you learn from every mistake you make, each time you will be one step closer to mastery.

I sincerely want to help you if you are serious about a successful career in sales. I will walk you through the *Don't Sell. Let Them Buy, Sales Conversation Process*. It's really a structure that gives you the freedom to focus on what your customers need and desire, so you can learn how best to serve them through your products and services. And, I'm here to tell you that this process, when consistently followed, can create a high six-figure income for you.

Notice I didn't say millions and millions of dollars. This process will do that too. But, let's get real. Most of you have no desire to create your own company and are happy to work for someone else who is willing to take on that burden.

So, that means that most of you work for companies that would never pay millions in salary. However, many companies are more than willing to pay in the high six-figures. But, they don't. Do you know why? Because, most of their reps don't do what it takes, or don't know how to do what it takes, to get to that next level of compensation.

At the beginning of my sales career, I was one of those reps. And, it makes me sick to think how much time I wasted, how much take-home pay I left on the table, and how much of my 401k didn't get matched. And, what's worse is how many customers I underserved. Is this you?

If you're stuck in a broken sales career and every morning you dread going to your job, or if you're a positive go-getter who is all over the place and just needs direction, then you're in the right place.

Even though each chapter builds on the one before, I've designed this book so you can choose any step of the *Don't Sell. Let Them Buy, Sales Conversation Process* to learn from and apply to your sales conversations.

Open your mind. Commit to being the success you know you can be and enjoy the ride.

The process you are about to learn, works!

Don't Sell. Let Them Buy. ™

## Chapter 1
### *Does Your Sales Career Make You Happy?*

Ugh…It's Monday morning after another pay period of falling short of your sales goal and, more embarrassingly, falling short of the company's minimum quota set for the two-week timeframe. Too many more underperformances like this and you'll be out.

Your company laptop is running slower than ever, so you're late logging onto the conference call for the regional-ra-ra-you-can-do-it-now-here-are-four-new-products-for-you-to-sell-meeting that happens at the beginning of every pay period.

You know the sales quotas are set way too high. You know that upper management has no clue as to what's really going on in the field. And, your sales are tanking. You lost the drive to win the company Incentive Trip to Italy. You're at the point where you just don't care. You're becoming more and more detached, less and less engaged with your responsibilities, your customers, and your company. Is this you? You're not alone.

# Chapter One

*According to a 2016 Gallup Poll on employee engagement, 32.6% of U.S. employees were "engaged" with their job, 50.7% were "not engaged," and 16.7% were "actively disengaged."[1]*

The term "engaged" refers to employees who are enthusiastically involved in their work and who are committed to their company and the customers they serve. How about you? What category best describes your level of engagement as an employee? How in the world did you get here?

Remember when you got that call inviting you in for an interview? You were so excited! You were so excited for the opportunity to work for such a great company. There were a lot of other sales people up for this position, but you landed it. You really liked your manager and team. (Well, there were a few odd ducks, but that's what makes great sales teams, right?) The drive wouldn't be too bad. Music and motivational books on Audible would help take your mind off the traffic. Your manager gave you a great territory. The rep before you barely penetrated the market, so you were primed to sell your socks off. The sales training was very comprehensive, but wow, there was a lot to learn in a short amount of time. But, that didn't bother you because you knew you could do it, and when you did, you would be earning a great income.

Your goals were pinned on the wall of your cubicle, front and center, so they were always in your face. You hit the street running with a positive-you-will-buy-from-me-because-I've-got-what-you-need-attitude. Management's expectations of you were high, and your expectations of your performance were even higher. You worked hard, hit your stride, and made your mark. You had this down.

Then, the company made a shift (a shift that to you seemed like a knee-jerk reaction to their competition) and began introducing new product after new product, expecting you to immediately incorporate them into your presentations and hit individual "product" quotas each pay period. Your prep time was getting longer and longer. Your customers began to see you as the guy on the TV infomercial who says, "But wait! There's more!" You became the thing that wouldn't leave.

Now, your account preparation has become so laborious that you only propose what you are familiar with. Your prep migrated from your office desk to the dashboard of your car, and you do it about 15 minutes before you walk in the customer's door. (Darn, it would have been a great idea to have that one marketing piece. Where did you put that thing anyway?)

In other words, the "new" has worn off. The little things that you never noticed before have become huge pain-in-the-neck obstacles. The amount of time invested in CRM is off the charts. Every time you turn around, your manager is asking for an update on your pipeline. (Twice a day! Really?) And, a few of the low-producing "odd ducks" have now become your lunch and water cooler buddies.

You and your misery-loves-company-buddies have about had it. There must be something better out there, and you're about ready to look for it.

Before you throw in the towel, know that all sales people have had times when they've felt so low that you couldn't scrape them off the floor with a spatula. I'm speaking from experience so stay with me.

I was first hired as a telephone sales rep who sold print yellow pages advertising (yes, Millennials, there are still printed phone books that are being used all over the world. Can you believe it?). When I began my sales career, I had no prior selling experience. In fact, I interviewed three times (going through gut-wrenching role play scenarios). Every time I was turned down, I was told, "You have the drive and the attitude but no experience. You're too much of a risk." I desperately wanted that job.

My dear friend, Nadine, who was a superstar telephone rep and who later became a sales trainer then district sales manager, spent hours training me. Had she not believed in me and spent the time working with me, I wouldn't have had the successful career I've had.

On a snowy Friday afternoon in February, I received a phone call from Cherry, my soon-to-be manager. She offered me the job but said I had to be on an airplane to Dallas on Sunday. I would be there for six weeks of Initial Sales Training. Had I had false teeth, they would have fallen out of my mouth. (Understand, I'm from the Midwest, and we have weird expressions so just go with me on this.) I was so excited, jumping up and down on the inside, and trying to maintain my composure on the outside. I asked how this happened, because I knew someone had already been hired. Cherry told me that the guy they offered the job to decided to stay on at his present job, and she was willing to take a chance on me. (No pressure there!)

At that time in my life, I had to make it. Failure was not an option. Sheer drive and naivete propelled me forward. I had no bad sales habits to break because I knew nothing about sales, so all they had to do was mold me. I was two years out of college with a teaching degree, but I had a great attitude, a strong work ethic, and an openness to learning what it took to be a success.

However, I wouldn't repeat those first years for anything. I spent a lot of time in the bathroom crying. I took rejection personally. It was God awful.

I remember having to stay late to call a plumber at 6:30 PM. His wife said she would tell him that I would be calling. He had a program in the phone book that was up for renewal, and I had two days left to close his advertising, or I had to pull it out of the book and take the loss on it.

I called, he answered, and as soon as I introduced myself, he came unglued. He yelled at me for calling him during his private time with his family. "How dare you!" And, on and on. I was reduced to a sobbing mess. When he realized that I was crying, he became quiet. I could hear his wife, in the background, trying to explain that she had forgotten to let him know that she had arranged the call. He apologized for his outburst and told me to go ahead and explain what I needed. So, there I was, a blubbering idiot and green as grass, trying to sound professional through my, "Wo, Wo, Would you tur, turn to pa, pa, page one hun, hundred an, and,four, four, forty-two, and lo, lo, look in the up, upper ri, right han, hand cor, corner to, to see, see your, your ad?" (OMG!)

My point is this. Everyone in sales starts on the bottom rung of the ladder. You did too. You weren't born knowing how to sell. You may have grown up with persuasion skills like my dad would say or manipulation skills like my mother preferred to say. I was my Dad's girl. I learned early on that, "Daddy, I really want this," didn't work well. However, "Daddy, I need this because…" worked like a charm. In my first three years, my sales were average to above average. I wasn't setting the world on fire, that's for sure. When my sales were down, I'd often blame the company for setting the sales goals too high.

## Chapter One

Never mind that the seasoned reps were hitting their targets, sailing passed sales goals, and winning the Incentive Trips and company awards. I wanted to be a part of that elite few, but I talked myself into believing that they had super powers that I didn't have.

Instead of objectively analyzing what was really going on, I spent less time prepping accounts and more time associating with other reps who were in worse slumps than me. And, I began to see my company as this huge, unfeeling behemoth that didn't care about its people. What a useless, senseless state I was in.

So, here's what it came down to. Karen, my telephone sales manager during my third to fifth year with the company, had the patience of a saint until she didn't. She would sit next to me and listen in on my calls with my customers. She would give feedback and guidance, but then she laid it all out in front of me.

"Chiq, you have everything it takes to be a top rep, but you have got to get out of your own way. Stop blaming everything around you and take responsibility for what you are doing to sabotage yourself. You've got to learn the steps of the sale, you have to know your product, and you have to continue to fail so you can finally get it right. It's okay to fall on your face. That's how you learn and remember what not to do the next time."

Then, she said, "Do you really think upper management wants you to fail so they can find another rep and spend thousands of dollars to get that new person ramped up to speed? Do you really think they don't know what they're doing? You need to take a step back to see how your thought process is affecting your performance and the way you feel about this company. This company is going to go on with or without you. The question is, are you going to step up and face what's going on here?"

Well, she got my attention. I was also embarrassed. I knew better. I was raised to take responsibility for my actions. I somehow got off track and lost my way. When we get ourselves in a downward spiral, we all need someone who has a mountain top view to help us see what we can't.

That was the beginning of what turned out to be my very lucrative sales career. But, I wouldn't repeat those beginning years for anything. Being on the bottom rung was not a rewarding place to be. So, what did I do next?

To get myself out of that mess, I first had to decide if the company I worked for was a good fit for me. If you are in the same place as I was then and you sincerely want help, then begin by taking an objective look at why this "stuff" is happening in the first place. And, learn the real reason that is causing your lack of sales and engagement with your job, company, and customers.

Below is the *Don't Sell. Let Them Buy, Commitment Check-In*. It is designed to help you determine your thought patterns, attitudes, and actions. Check in to see where you stand.

For the following topic areas, rank your response on a scale of one to ten, "10" being the highest. Where do you stand?

**Don't Sell. Let Them Buy, Commitment Check-In:**

**How you feel about your company?** How would you rank:

- \_\_\_\_ Your company among all others in your industry?
- \_\_\_\_ How proud you are to let others know that you work for this company?
- \_\_\_\_ The passion you have for this industry?
- \_\_\_\_ How much your company appreciates you?
- \_\_\_\_ How fulfilling your job is as a career?

_____ The opportunities available for you to make your desired income?

**How you feel about the products and services you represent?** How would you rank:

_____ Your products and services among those of your competitors?

_____ Your level of passion when presenting your products and services to your customers?

**How you feel about the customers who buy your products and services?** How would you rank:

_____ Your level of passion for the customers that buy your products or services?

If your score is anything less than "10," you do have a problem. But, before you decide to look for employment elsewhere, keep reading.

Is the company you work for that out of whack? The products and services that substandard and the customers that off-putting?

Could there be something you're doing, or not doing, that is influencing your attitude and lowering your level of passion and engagement?

Let's assess the latter first. There's one more *Don't Sell. Let Them Buy*, *Commitment Check-In* that needs your attention. Take a breath, and be honest with yourself.

**How you feel about your efforts as an employee?** How would you rank:

_____ Your effort towards learning all you can about your company, its history, and mission?

_____ Your effort towards becoming a knowledge expert in your company's products and services?

_____ Your effort towards learning how to successfully educate your customers about your products and services?

_____ Your effort towards overcoming customer concerns and brush-offs?

_____ Your effort to seek advice from the top reps in your company?

_____ Your effort towards mastering the fundamental steps of the sales conversation?

If your score is "10" on every one of these questions, yet your sales are tanking, and you're not happy or fulfilled, then perhaps this job is just not for you.

It's time to be honest and do yourself, your company, and teammates a favor - quit and find a career that you love. Make it your intention to serve others every day, doing something that gives you joy and purpose.

If your score is less than "10" on every one of these questions, hit yourself upside the head like I did and get a clue, Sherlock. The issue may not be with your company but with you. Try the following for one month, and see what happens.

### *Don't Sell. Let Them Buy, Nuggets:*

1. **Take responsibility for your actions or inactions and the success you create or don't create.**

    - To blame is unproductive.
    - To learn from making bad choices is priceless.

2. **Seek out a mentor.**

    - Ask the two most successful reps to have coffee with you.
    - Discover what they do, what makes them successful, and what makes them want to engage with the job, the company, and their customers.
    - Ask to ride with them so that you can see them in action with a customer.
    - Hang with the successful people, and stay away from the influence of the negative naysayers.
    - Do what the successful reps do, and try it for yourself.

3. **Commit to yourself and your company.**

    - Remember, every sales rep starts on the bottom rung of the ladder.
    - The amount of success achieved is directly related to the amount of effort you invest.

If you decide it is "you" who needs an adjustment, follow the advice above then retake the Check-In after one month, to see how your attitude and level of commitment to your company changed. This works. As Wayne Dyer, American philosopher, self-help author, and motivational speaker said, *"Change the way you look at things, and the things you look at change."*[2]

You must believe that your company is the competition and sets the standard in your industry for the products and services it delivers. If you don't, you'll always be playing the comparison game and always be feeling resentful because you see your company as somehow lacking. Your customers will see this, which means your paycheck will reflect it.

When you believe in yourself, "engage" with your company, and put effort into being prepared with product knowledge as well as great listening, selling and "serving" skills, you can focus on discovering what your customers really want. They will see your commitment to your products and services from your passion.

This is where customer trust comes in. When this happens, customers will buy from you, your productivity will increase, and you will help your customers and yourself experience a better way of life. And, isn't that what we all want?

When you see your company as a "10," you embrace and protect its image. You become an extension of your company. The way you represent your products and services takes on an air of strength and stability, attributes that customers are willing to invest in. When all the above happens, that is when you know you and your employer are a good match. I discovered that my company and I were a good match. I am very grateful for my 22 years of employment.

And, I am indebted to Karen, my manager, who believed in me when I didn't. She took the time to get me on the right path. She even threatened to tear up my paycheck if I didn't take advantage of the matching 401K program. And, 30 years later, I can say I am glad that I listened to her.

Post Script: At the beginning of this chapter I mentioned that your computer is running slowly, because for over two months now, you have ignored the memo from the IT department asking you to make an appointment so they could do a system update.

In fact, that memo warned you this would happen. I believe this falls under *Don't Sell. Let Them Buy Nugget #1: Take responsibility for your actions or inactions and the success you create or don't create.*

Chapter One

# Just sayin'...

[1.] **Adkins, Amy**. (2016). U.S. Employee Engagement Steady in June. *Workplace,* Gallup Daily, June 1-30. Retrieved from **http://www.gallup.com/poll/193901/employee-engagement-steady-june.aspx?g_source=Employee+engagement+2016&g_medium=search&g_campaign=tiles**

[2.] **Dyer, Wayne. (n. d.).** Wayne's Blog. [Web log post] Success Secrets. Retrieved from **http://www.drwaynedyer.com/blog/success-secrets/**

Don't Sell. Let Them Buy.™

## Chapter 2

## *How to Earn the Right to Ask the Customer to Buy from You*

I am going to begin this chapter by admitting that I never liked doing account preparation. Every customer required dedicated prep time. It was the same thing over and over, blah, blah, blah. OMG! What an idiot I was. My attitude and focus were fixed in the wrong direction and on all the wrong things.

I foolishly undervalued account preparation. I saw it as work, as drudgery, instead of a path forward. I was so focused on my weekly, mandated sales target that I forgot the most important factor – how to best showcase my products to my customers so they would "naturally" want to say, "Yes!"

Then, when I was in my third year of telephone sales, Karen (my manager) hit me over the head with a proverbial two-by-four. After her "comin' to Jesus" talk, I realized:

- how much money I was leaving on the table,
- how many sales contests I was losing,
- how much I was underserving my customer,

- how embarrassed I was to be an average producer,
- how unorganized I was,
- how stressed I was,
- and, I was causing all this unrest myself.

Think about your situation. If you're in the same boat that I was, you need to know that land is right in front of you. You just need to get out of your own way to see it. Since I've lived this experience, I can show you how.

Let's say that you're committed to your company, its products, and its services. And, you're committed to serving the customers who are just waiting for you to call them.

Don't you dare roll your eyes. I know what you're thinking; I thought the same thing. But, there are millions of business owners out there who want and need what you have to offer. You just need to find out who and where they are. And, just because you find these buyers doesn't mean you deserve to be in front of them. Now, what do I mean by that?

Ask yourself, "Am I really committed to creating a successful, lucrative career in sales?" If you truly believe you are, then know this:

The *Don't Sell. Let Them Buy, Sales Conversation Process*, no matter what you are selling, is directly related to the amount of effort you put into earning the right to ask for the sale.

I'm talking about your level of commitment to the preparation you do before making a sales call. It took me too long to figure this out. When I did, I was on my way and finally attained a consistent, high six-figure income.

Here's a scenario that takes place every day in the lives of most average to below average producing sales people.

Congratulations! You finally got the prospect to give you an appointment! That's huge! Now, what do you do? It's 4:30 PM. Your appointment is at 10 AM the day after tomorrow. And, tomorrow is a day packed full of seeing customers.

Those golf clubs are calling to you from the trunk of your car, aren't they?

And, for you, so are those gorgeous shoes from Nordstrom. You can hear them just flapping in their box. They can't wait to get on your feet.

It seems that you're left with a choice. Do you celebrate? (Nothing really, because all you have is the appointment. You haven't sold anything yet.) Or, do you stay and prep for this customer, whose conversion could put you closer to your goal of winning the company Incentive Trip to Paris?

Then, you justify it and tell yourself:

"I make money when I'm in the field and in front of the customer – not at my desk prepping for the appointment. How can I possibly know what to prep until I get in front of the customer and have a conversation with them? I know what I need to say. I can think on my feet. I can squeeze in the account prep this time tomorrow and still get my daughter to the soccer game at six."

And, you choose to go to the golf course or Nordstrom.

The next day ran longer than anticipated making you late in getting your daughter to the soccer game. You planned to prep last night, but you got so wrapped up in that great movie on TV.

One thing lead to another so before your big appointment the following morning, you only had time to do the dashboard/armrest prep. How'd that work for ya?

## Chapter Two

This is not an example of making a mistake. It is an example of making a clear choice. You chose to put other things before prepping to see your customer the following day. Over the years, I have learned that everything we act upon or do comes down to a choice, and every choice has a consequence. Good, bad, whatever.

I believe in taking responsibility for my actions, and therefore I hold myself accountable to a high standard. When I finally learned this, my managers never had to put pressure on me because I put enough pressure on myself. If a sale didn't work out, I stopped blaming the customer. I stopped to analyze what I could have done to lose the sale. Most of the time, it was because I wasn't prepared or didn't do my homework before the sales call.

In this scenario, your choice resulted in money left on the table, a lost sale, and a potential customer's lost respect – who by the way could have referred you to new customers. More importantly, you know you let your company, you customer, and yourself down. That's a crummy feeling, isn't it? I know because I made this choice many times and felt terrible afterward. Oh, and that trip to Paris is no closer.

Bottom line: if you don't put in the effort, you can't expect to get much in return. Nor, do you deserve it, because you did not earn the right to be there in the first place.

And, you should know that your choice to be unprepared speaks volumes to your customer. They can see right through your lack of preparedness. *"What's wrong with this company that they don't train their people and let them on the street to waste my time. If they don't put enough energy into getting the right reps, their products must not be any good either. And, if the rep isn't prepared or knowledgeable, then they don't take their job seriously, and they certainly won't take care of me."*

You may have amazing conversation skills and know how to engage with the customer. But, you quickly discover that when you have the potential for a huge sale, for which you can't answer critical questions because you didn't do your homework, you've just wasted your time and the customer's time. Now, you have to back out of the call to do what you should have done in the first place – prepare. The momentum you had during the call has stalled, and what could have been a one-call sales conversation just turned into an unnecessary two-call sales conversation or worse, a lost sale. Why?

On your next visit, the customer may not be in a buying mood, they don't give you the time they were going to give on the first visit, they thought about what you have to offer and decided to pass altogether, or the competition swooped in and stole them away.

If you can relate, try this….

**Have a face-to-face with yourself and find your gratitude.**

- Give thanks that you have been hired by an amazing company that produces products and services you are proud to represent.
- Be grateful that your manager saw something in you when you interviewed for the position, something that you somehow lost. Find it.
- Realize that it is your passion and determination to do what it takes that will turn you into your own success story.
- Believe you can and you will.

**Stop, look at your habits and check in with yourself.**

- Why don't I put effort into consistent preparation?

- What am I doing that is holding me back?
- How can I become an expert in my products and services?
- Who should I talk with to give me insight?
- Know that every superstar sales rep started at the lowest rung of the ladder. They became superstars because they chose to commit themselves to the learning process and then worked to become experts.
- Commit to do the same and fly up that ladder!

**Become an expert in product knowledge.**

- When you become an expert in your products and services, your confidence and passion come through during your presentations.
- You can think more clearly, answer more thoughtfully, and speak more directly. This builds customer trust.
- A customer's trust in you leads them to buy from you.
- Commit to becoming an expert in your product knowledge, and reap the rewards in sales commissions, company awards, and customer loyalty.

**Give each customer dedicated preparation and focus.**

- Treat each customer's account as you would want a rep to do for you.
- Earn your customer's attention, and discover inventive ways to serve them with your products and services. When you do, you will sell larger programs as well as more products and services.
- Your confidence level will increase and so will your commissions.

## Seek the advice of sales superstars.

- Ask a few superstars to have a coffee and conversation with you.
- High producing reps love to give their knowledge away, because they know that's the secret to success.
- When you stop thinking about your pocketbook, you can do as Zig Ziglar said, *"You can get everything in life you want if you will just help enough other people get what they want."*[1]

**Here are some other ways to help you make a solid commitment to account preparation.**

## Time block your week.

- Carve out specific mornings, afternoons, or whatever amount of preparation time is needed for your product or service, and stick to it.
- Time-blocking will:
    - Help you concentrate.
    - Keep you organized.
    - Give you more freedom during your sales day.
    - Allow you to get more done.
    - Put your attitude in a better place.

## Prep as many accounts as you can in that time block.

- This allows you to be ready to see that customer, who canceled on you last week, at any available moment in time.
- Realize that, as you build your presentations, you can use the same prep for other customers.

- This saves you time, and you're seen as an expert because your presentation will be honed to perfection.

**During prepping time:**

- Avoid your email.
- Let your phone calls go to voicemail.
- Don't visit with your colleagues.
- Schedule your calls around your account preparation.
- If you have a customer that can see you tomorrow, but you're not ready, don't shoot yourself in the foot and take the appointment. Don't take the appointment until you have **earned the right** to be in front of them by doing their account preparation first.

**Commit to doing thorough account preparation, and you will:**

- Earn the right to ask the customer to buy.
- Sell bigger programs (more products and services).
- Be perceived by your customer as an expert in your industry.
- Be more likely to be referred to new leads by your customers.
- Win more company sales contests.
- Be perceived as a superstar among management and your colleagues.
- Be on your way to a high six-figure income.

## Summary:

- Commit to your company that you will represent its products and services in the best possible light.

- Commit to your customers that you will prepare, earn the right to ask them to buy your products and services, and always serve them by recommending the best solutions for their needs, for the right reasons.

- Commit to yourself that you will time block your work week to ensure that the right amount of prep time is available to guarantee your company, your customer, and you a better way of life.

When you do your research, learn all you can about your potential customer and understand how your products and services can help them; you will have earned the right to ask them to buy from you. In other words, you reap when you prep.

---

[1.] **Ziglar, Zig.** Secrets of Closing the Sale. Grand Rapids, Michigan: Revell.

## Chapter 3

### *How to Prepare*
### *Don't Sell. Let Them Buy, Sales Conversations*

Think like a business owner. Try this on for size. Think of yourself as the owner of your own business, whether you are employed by a small or megacorporation. Assume the mindset that you are working for yourself. The customers in your territory are your sole responsibility.

When you hold yourself accountable to them, the buck stops with you; you become protective of their account, and you focus on providing the best possible customer service. They, in turn, will remain loyal and continue to reward you by listening to what you have to say and purchasing the recommendations you make. You become the one who has the most influence over customer loyalty.

When you take responsibility, a shift in your thinking occurs. When issues arise, you stop blaming the company and the departments that serve you.

## Chapter Three

You become more detailed when submitting paperwork and uploading digital submissions. Your communication with other departments improves, resulting in fewer errors and more accurate, possibly faster fulfillment.

You will be seen as a professional with integrity and high standards – a representative that truly cares about their clients. Most of your support team will automatically step up and process your accounts with more care and attention.

When this happens, be sure to show gratitude to the employees who went the extra mile for you. They deserve to know they are appreciated, and they will be more likely to continue to help you in the future. Not only that, but they will also welcome your work because they know your level of care and detail will make their job easier. Be the rep that everyone wants to help.

When I adopted this mindset and assumed responsibility for my actions, I became a positive, can-do, top sales representative who earned the respect of her customers as well as her management. I found that when situations came up, I didn't wait for someone else to fix it. I took responsibility and found the solutions instead of complaining, blaming others, and doing nothing.

I am very grateful for my 22 consecutive years with my employer. They took a chance on me, supported me, and trained me. They awarded me with unit, division and company awards, sending me on amazing sales Incentive Trips that gave me the opportunity to see fascinating parts of the world.

I have many wonderful friends, including Rachel (my last manager) who put up with my, "No. I'm not going to sell that thing to my customers.

It makes no sense and doesn't work." Her dedication to doing what is right is why Rachel and I are such good friends.

Then, there were the late nights in the office when many of my teammates – Mary Ann, Scott, Barry, Tony and I – would be trying to enter data into what we called "Intel-e-hell," the newly customized CRM system. The air was blue, mostly around my desk, from the choice words I would spew from frustration. But, the company was supportive. I remember, one evening, I called the Help Desk and was transferred to a young woman in Canada. I heard all this racket in the background. It was 9 PM her time, and she was at a bar having drinks with friends. She was a trooper. She stayed on the phone with me, helping me navigate through a maze of unfamiliar territory until I successfully entered my customer's new program into the system.

And, then there was Mark, a wonderful colleague, and rep in my division. He would leave around 5:30 PM to enjoy family time and dinner; and, then he would come back around 7 PM, in his PJs, to continue making sense of "Intel-e-hell" until about 10 PM. Oh, the memories. I digress.

After 22 years of working for this corporation, an opportunity came my way that was, at that time in my life, a better fit. I was hired at a competing corporation. As a Key Accounts Executive, I was part of a unit of six reps and a manager. We handled the major, high-billing accounts. I must say that, in the beginning, it was lonely and just plain odd.

## Chapter Three

The redeeming factors were Wanda (my manager), my customers and my buddies – Barry, Scott, and Lee Ann – who also migrated to this company. Thank God for them! Nothing rattles Wanda. She was the best manager I have ever worked for and the best salesperson I have ever seen in action. I have tremendous gratitude for her allowing me to be a part of her team. Even though Wanda wanted to strangle me at times, she let me be me. I was a handful because my customers always came first.

Don't get me wrong. I was very loyal to my company. However, I would not sell something that was not in the best interests of my customers, not even if it was mandatory to do so. Nope. Was not going to happen. I assumed sole responsibility for the customers in my territory. It was my integrity and their livelihood on the line, which I took very seriously.

If you are asked to sell something where the company fulfillment of that something is less than stellar, are you going to put your reputation on the line and possibly do harm to your customer's business? I believe in holding the company accountable for accurate, fully functioning fulfillment. If I didn't, I would have had only myself to blame. Not only that, but I would have failed my customers causing them to doubt my word when I came to them with new products in the future. I certainly wouldn't have looked to them as sources of referrals either. Still, I digress.

My point is this. It is very rare that salespeople find themselves in a union environment. This seems counter-intuitive, but that is exactly what I walked into. To this day, I have the work ethic of putting in however many hours it takes to do my job. That's why I'm usually the first one in the office and the last to leave.

About six months after being hired, a guy in my unit pulled me aside and said, "You need to stop with the hours you're putting in and selling so much. You're changing the dynamic around here and raising the budgets for all of us." If I had false teeth, they would have fallen on the floor. I looked him straight in the eye, quickly bit my tongue, plastered a smile on my face, and said, "I'll be happy to show you what I do. Do you need help?" He walked away.

I was a new employee in a foreign, "union" environment, who thought it better to keep to myself. I was the black sheep. I was there to make money, but I had my head in the right frame of mind. I knew that I could make money by helping my customers have a better way of life through the company solutions I offered.

So, I focused on getting up to speed, learning all the ins and outs of the products I was going to sell, especially the new online product with all of its add-ons. Oh yes, the rate sheets and promotions had to be mastered as well. What fun. The rate sheets and incentive programs changed as frequently as you changed your underwear.

After numerous tries, I finally developed an easy-to-understand, engaging and repeatable way of prepping, in order to educate my customers about my products, services, and creating and presenting recommendations to my customers. This learning took months of focus, dedication, and lots of self-talk and Wanda-talk. Prepping each account took a lot of time until it didn't anymore; because I had it down and I had made it organic. And, did it ever pay off!

By the end of my second year, I was the top producing online rep in the company, and I held that position for five consecutive years. I was making a lot of money.

A few reps complained to management that I couldn't be selling on the up and up, so they did a background investigation of everything I had sold. I was mortified, hurt, and infuriated all at the same time. My reputation was being questioned. As it turned out, management complimented me on my production. They confirmed that all of my customers were happy with my service and their programs.

Management also asked if I would consent to be filmed, so I could share how I prepped and shared the online product to the rest of the sales teams across the country. I was thrilled to help. My presentation was sent to every region in the country and incorporated into the new-hire training program as well.

What I did was not extraordinary. It was simply learning my products until I owned them. It was also, and at all times, keeping the best interests of my customers first and making sure that I did my best to serve them with what I had to offer. When I served my customers, I was rewarded – maybe not at that particular time, but everything always seemed to work out.

Yes, I was constantly mindful of what I was expected to produce in sales, but when I focused on the needs of the customer, my sales results reflected my service to them.

Also important was establishing a solid, repeatable preparation and recommendation process – a process that set me up for a positive outcome. This will be covered in the pages to follow.

### How Well Do You Know Your Products and Services?

If your product knowledge does not rank a "10," ten being the highest, then do your job and learn your trade! You cannot earn the right to be in front of a potential client if you aren't an expert in your industry.

**Analyze your recommendations.**

Are you in a rut? Do you find yourself constantly recommending the same program because that's what you know? YOU are holding yourself back, and you are cheating your customers from the benefits of what your company has to offer.

Become an expert and learn everything you can offer your customers. You will have more clients, clients that will continually look to you for answers, and your sales production will increase.

**Take time to talk with the highest producing, most respected reps in your company.**

- What products and services are they consistently selling?
- How are they selling them?
- Why are they selling them?
- What do they know that you don't?
- Whom do they recommend you get to know in the different departments to process your work?
- What is their approach to account preparation?
- What are the industry stories they've discovered that have opened doors to more sales?
- What is their secret to sales success?

Most really successful people, in any industry, are more than willing to help a struggling colleague. They were once in the same shoes. You can bet that someone gave them helpful advice along the way and all because they asked for help.

I can't impress upon you more that talking with people who have "been there, done that" is one of the best ways to learn how to increase your knowledge and sales production. You don't have to suffer in silence. They've seen it all. This one conversation will also change your attitude and give you the direction you need.

**Know your products and services.**

You should know every product and service your company offers. You need to know what products do well and which ones don't. You also need to become an expert in enthusiastically educating your customers about every feature and every benefit of those products and services.

**Form an Alliance with Key Players in the Marketing Department.**

I am well aware that in companies of all sizes the right hand doesn't always know what the left hand is doing. Furthermore, many times, marketing departments will develop products and programs that, by the time they are presented to the sales team, make no sense; because, those products and programs were born in an alternate universe that is far from real-world experience.

Management is all gung-ho about the thought of a new revenue stream, and they expect their sales team to warmly embrace and sell the living daylights out of these products.

However, many times, the sale team is completely mystified, because they know what is really happening in the field and are befuddled as to why their input was left out of the equation. This creates animosity between departments, breeding negativity, lack of sales production, and low morale.

On the other hand, it is the job of the marketing department to keep the company on the cutting edge, so it continues to BE the competition and not simply a part of the competition. Their hearts are in the right place, but management must ensure the marketing department works with the sales team.

If the team is not behind new products, those products will not be made to the customer, and no one wins. Well, I got that out of my system.

However, as I stated in Chapter 1 when you see your company as a "10," you embrace and protect its image. You become an extension of your company. The way you represent your products and services takes on an air of strength and stability, attributes that customers are willing to invest in.

With all of that said, you have customers out there who are waiting for you to give them a better way of life with your products and services. You can't do that unless you have complete product knowledge. Do you?

Here is a checklist to help you become a product knowledge expert for your company.

### Steps to Learning Your Products and Services

### What is the basic product or service that you sell?

- Learn the purpose of it and understand its benefits.
- What are the different programs you can offer?
- What are the circumstances in which you would offer one over the other?
- What program is right for which customer?
- Learn how to effectively communicate your products, their features, and benefits.

- Know how to quickly locate these products on your rate sheet.

**What are the add-on products? (These are products or services that complement or add value to the basic product.)**

- What is their purpose? Understand their features and benefits.
- When is the right time to add them to a customer's program?
- Who is the right customer for these products?
- Learn how to effectively communicate what they are, their features, and benefits.
- Know how to quickly locate these products on your rate sheet.

**Create a checklist. That way, when you are prepping, you will remember to review all items, in the same order, every time. Why?**

- You will soon find yourself picking up speed because this repetition will become second nature.
- You will become an expert on your products and services.
- You won't leave money on the table.
- You will be in a great position to provide the best solution for your customers.

**When new products are introduced:**

- Keep an open mind. Believe that management knows where it wants to go and has the best interests in mind for its employees and customers. Management is always looking for new revenue streams and ways to improve its bottom line. And, yes, management is great at disrupting the selling patterns of its reps. Understand that disruptions are a part of the job. Accept this fact and focus on serving your customers.
- Immediately review the new products and learn how they can benefit your customers.
- If they are a benefit, incorporate them into your account preparation. Be the first on your team to sell these new products, and you'll be seen as a role model by your teammates as well as management. Your customers will be on the cutting edge as well.
- If you can't see their benefits to your customers, talk to your manager, marketing rep or another sales rep you respect to see what you may be missing.

By committing to memory what you have to offer, completely understanding why and when you should offer it, you will be able to think on your feet. You will be able to change your recommendation on a dime, if necessary, even right in front of the customer and you won't miss a beat. That is what a true expert does. But, this can only be done if you first have the desire to be the best you can be in your industry and commit the time to learning all there is to know about your products and services.

Chapter Three

## Sales Success Begins with Thorough Account Preparation

Have you noticed everything around you that successfully works does so because its function is based on a proven repetitive pattern?

To turn on your cell phone, create a successful online conference call or get your dog to settle down, there are certain steps that, when followed, lead to success. (Note: My dog will do anything for his broccoli and jicama bowl – which is his after-dinner dessert.)

The opposite is also true. You can't put today's manufactured cars in reverse without first turning them on. Grandma's sugar cookies won't taste good if you accidentally substitute salt for sugar (like I did my first time making them at eight years old). Your husband won't take out the garbage unless you ask him once and remind him two more times. Generally.

**Commit to Learning the Process.**

To become successful at sales is no different. When I committed myself to following a consistent format or sequence of steps, I noticed a marked improvement in my productivity and sales ability. I realized sales success follows the same format, without fail and for every customer, beginning with account preparation and ending with all nine steps of the sales conversation. This concept works.

Let me explain why this works and show you how to create a successful, repetitive structure for your account preparation – regardless of what you are selling.

**The *Don't Sell. Let Them Buy*, Repetitive Prepping Process Allows You To:**

- Consistently perform thorough account preparation.
- Save time.
- Stay organized.
- Learn what is in your sales arsenal.
- Learn to quickly locate all important documents. Become a product knowledge expert in your industry.
- Learn the trends in your customer's industry.
- Become confident and prepared.
- Look professional and in control to your customers.
- Sell bigger and better programs.
- Increase your productivity.

Next are the steps of account preparation that will give you the knowledge to create powerful recommendations. Your recommendations will answer the needs and wants of your customers with your products and services.

At first glance, this will look overwhelming. Almost everything is when you are learning something new. Remember when you first learned to drive a car? Okay, that was too far back to remember. Wait. Do you have a driver's license? If not, how about when you had to learn your company's new computer system? Was the air blue around your cubicle?

Oh, yes, let's not forget that CRM system that is supposed to keep you in the field and in front of the customer. How's that working out for you?

**Prepare to SERVE.**

Well, guess what? This is so much easier. It can be fun and rewarding if you want it to be.

## Chapter Three

It's all in your mindset. Prepare to SERVE, and you will RECEIVE in return. Once you get the hang of it, you will follow the same steps for every account; the process will become organic, and you will move quickly. Depending on what you're selling, this prep should take you no more than 20 to 30 minutes per account. The more time you put into the front end of the sales call, the more success you will have in the end.

Begin to serve by doing your homework, which means learning everything you can about your customer before having that first in-depth conversation. The more you let your new client know that you have taken the time to learn about them and their company, the more they will like, trust, and listen to you. When they listen, they will be open to what you have to say.

**Earn the Right to be Given an Audience with a Customer.**

So, let's set the foundation for success by first earning the right to be given an audience with a potential customer. Shift your mindset away from your pocketbook (that's Mid-West talk again), sales goal or company objective.

Shift your mindset instead to learning about your client and how you, your products, and services can help them have a better way of life.

The following is an outline for Account Preparation Strategy for you to apply. The following strategy is for prepping existing accounts in your territory, accounts that you previously created from a cold call or accounts you may have inherited from another rep. The strategy is directed at selling digital products so you can learn what to look for when analyzing a customer's website.

It doesn't matter what you are selling. The steps of Account Preparation are basically the same. What differs is if the customer is an existing customer or a potential client. All the steps need to be incorporated, but the amount of deep-dive attention will vary.

## Account Preparation Strategy

### Company and Contact Information Review:

#### Name of company:
- Note unusual spelling.
- Is this a privately-owned company or a franchise? This could make a difference on who the real decision-maker is.

#### Address:
- You will want to handle this account when you have others in the same vicinity to cut down on drive-time.

#### Name and confirmation of authorizing party:
- Note unusual spelling. Are the notes on the account correct? Look for signatures on past contracts to make sure.
- What is this person's title? You want to work with the decision-maker.
- Just because the rep last year worked with the secretary (whose signature is noted as last year's signatory) doesn't mean you shouldn't work with the CEO or Director this year.

#### Payment status:
- If delinquent, learn and follow company procedure.
- Speak with the Credit Representative assigned to the account to bring you up-to-speed.

- If this is a new customer for you, check to see if they are actually a past customer that has been canceled because of failure to pay their bill.

*(There's nothing like finding a new prospect who's really excited to see you. You prepare your socks off, they accept your amazing recommendation, you submit the account for processing, and you are informed that the customer owes the company a lot of money. This means they have to pay what they owe and will probably need to come up with money up front before you can close the account. If you ALWAYS check the payment status of the account, this may not happen. I say "may not" because there are always those that work the system by changing their business name and phone number in an attempt to look like a new customer. At least you can save yourself a lot of frustration and wasted time by not walking blissfully into bad debt nightmares.)*

**Delinquency is not a reason to skip account preparation.**

- Always give the customer the benefit of the doubt. Be kind. You would want this type of treatment if the situation were reversed.
- The point is to serve with your heart as much as with your head. This keeps your mind open to solutions that will help your customer through a rough time – sickness, death in the family, the previous rep dropped the ball, the product didn't perform, or the customer lost a large client.
- Look at the account payment history. Is this the first time the customer has been delinquent or is this a pattern? The point is to enlighten yourself, so you will know exactly what you are walking into.

## Set the Appointment:

## STOP! Before you go any further:

- Call and set an appointment with all necessary decision-makers. In today's world, a lot of decisions are made by a committee.
- Once you speak to the person, who authorizes the "blank," (insert whatever makes sense for your industry here) be sure to ask, "Who besides yourself is also a part of this decision and needs to attend our meeting?"
- The goal is to meet with all necessary parties at once.

## However, what if you discover the company:

- Is out of business?
- Was bought out by another company and it's not your account anymore?
- Is now a franchise and you can't work with franchise accounts?
- Moved out of your territory?
- Is in bankruptcy?
- Owner has just died?
- Has just suffered a fire, flood or (God help us) an earthquake?
- The point is – don't get wrapped up in account prep unless you have validated that the company is still in business and the decision-makers will meet with you.

## Account Review (if it's an existing customer and the account is up for renewal):

## Note the current billing:

- Is this the full billing, or was there an adjustment on the account because of an error or customer service issue?

**Study the customer's current program:**
- What products or services do they have?
- Are the products and services up-to-date?
- How long has the customer had this product or service?
- If applicable and if this is a new customer in your territory, you will want to pull all reports that give you access to the performance of their current products or services. For example, if you are selling a digital product (such as SEO) whose performance can be measured, you will want to be prepared with a solution when you discover the product has been underperforming. Trust me, if this is the case, the customer will tell you on the phone that they are not happy and want to cancel when you call to schedule an appointment,
- If this is a current customer of yours, I hope I don't have to inform you that you should be doing a monthly review of their product performance.

    This is the only way to be on top of any issues and establish a continuous-stay-in-front-of-this-potential-issue conversation with your customer.

**Customer Website Review (if you're prepping for a new and existing customer):**

The example below applies to those reps who sell products and services in the online arena; but, this process can certainly be applied to any customer. Why? Because, a company's website is their virtual business card. It is their digital brochure.

- Is the website up-to-date? Look at the very bottom of any page. If it doesn't have the current year next to the copyright, this is telling. It indicates that your customer is either not Internet savvy or doesn't have a person on their payroll handling their website and social media needs.
- What customers say on their site and how they express it, as well as what they don't say, tells a story of how much they understand or don't understand about the power of a website.
- The message communicated on a website is often a potential customer's first impression. If it is not engaging, clear, comprehensive, easy to navigate, or lacks the "connection" factor (makes it easy for the customer to make contact), the site has failed. That means it definitely is not a source of powerful lead generation.
- On the other hand, the company could be very profitable; because, it has established itself in the marketplace as the competition by relying on its provision of exceptional personal contact, excellent customer experience, and outstanding products.

The point I'm making is "not to judge a book by its cover." Be observant, be open, and look for holes to fill. Look for ways to serve your customer through your products and services. You may have the answer that they don't realize they have a need for yet.

- What is the website communicating and is the communication effective?
  - What is the main message? Is it clear? Is the copy, content, and "searchable" rich?
  - Does the copy engage and connect with potential customers?
  - Who are their customers?

- - Who could be their customers if their message was adjusted?
  - What can you learn about the company, its products, and services?
  - What are the areas of strength?
  - What are the areas of needed improvement?
  - Click on all tabs; look for ways your products and services will take their company to a more profitable position.
- What is the offer or "ask?"
  - Is there one?
  - Is it clear and enticing?
- How easy is it for a potential customer to engage with this company?
  - Can you talk to a person?
  - How easy is it to find the company phone number and email address?
- Are there testimonials?
  - How old are they?
  - What do they really say about the company?
- Are there blogs?
  - Read them!
  - What can you learn about the customer?
  - What can you learn about their industry trends?

**Online Reviews and Ratings:**

- Yelp.
- Google.
- Facebook (their company Facebook).

- If the reviews are good, what is the primary positive feedback and what is it about – the service, an individual, or the products?
- If the reviews are bad, what are the primary negative issues? Where is the breakdown?
- Has the company taken the time to respond to the reviews? If not, make a note to alert your customer. They may not be monitoring the reviews and would jump at the chance to make things right.

**Did you know:**

*46% of online customers expect brands to provide customer service on Facebook - Source: Oracle Retail*[1]

*83% of complaints that received a reply on social media liked or loved the fact that the company responded – Source: Bain & Co*[2]

*88% of consumers are less likely to buy from companies that leave unanswered complaints on social media – Source: Countersocial*[3]

**Customer Profiles:**

- LinkedIn.
- Facebook.
- Get to know another side of your customer.
    - Where did they go to school?
    - How long have they worked for their employer?
    - What are their interests?
- Look for common ground.

**Study Your Customer's Product:**
- You don't need to be an expert in the customer's products, nor is it wise to imply that you know more than you do. However, you should take the time to learn enough to ask thought-provoking questions that will demonstrate you are trying to understand their world.
- This effort will show that you care. A demonstration of care leads to trust, open communication, and (most likely) a sale and a new valued customer.

**Study Your Customer's Industry:**
- Bring new information and new insight to the conversation.
  - The web is full of information. Look at blog posts and websites; go to your customer's LinkedIn profile and see who they are following.
  - What are the most up-to-date trends in their industry?
  - What can you share that is new and captures the interest of your customer?
- Knowing your customer is one thing, but it's vital that you understand what their market is doing, where it's heading, and how your customer fits into the mix.
- Look for sales stories and testimonials on the web that exhibit success, because these businesses are progressive and staying ahead of the curve.

Now, you're ready to create no less than two well thought-out recommendations. I know exactly what you're thinking. How can I possibly come up with even one recommendation if I haven't even spoken to the decision-maker?

## Open your mind and look at what you've learned.

**You know:**
- What the customer does.
- Who the customer serves.
- What the customer sells.
- What the industry trends are for the customer's products.
- What your products and services can do for this customer.
- That every business is interested in:
  - Increasing sales.
  - Reducing cost.
  - Increasing performance.
  - Improving quality.
  - Reducing turnover.
  - Improving their customer experience.

This is the fun part!

You have confirmed an appointment for 10 AM with your newest potential client. The only conversation you've had with them was to set the appointment, and you've never physically been to their place of business. You know the program they currently have with your company (or if they don't have one at all), and you've gone through the website checklist outlined above. You also have your industry knowledge and know what your products and services can do for a business like this new client. So, go for it!

Create no less than two recommendations for them to consider.

"But, I don't know what they need! How can I do this?" you whine.

Oh, for crying out loud. You don't need to know anything else right now. You know your products and services. You know which ones excel as well as which ones to refrain from offering because they have bugs or issues.

You also have a good idea of how your products can fit into that client's business by looking at their website. Plus, you know the industry. Give it your best shot.

## When You Know Your Products, You Can Change Directions on a Dime.

It doesn't matter that your recommendations may not hit the mark. Why?

Because when you get in the habit of doing this for every customer who is willing to take the time to see you, your product knowledge will become organic and you will become an expert. You will be able to change directions on a dime and use those recommendations as the foundation for what you decide to offer – right on the spot. Plus, you further engage the customer. You get them involved in creating the right solution when you make your recommendations. I will get more into this when we get to Chapter 9 *Step 5: Recommendation "How to Present Your Don't Sell. Let Them Buy, Recommendations."*

**Why create two recommendations?**

You are demonstrating to the customer that you:

- Gave thought to their business. You did your homework.
- Know how your products can benefit their business.
- Came prepared so as not to waste their time.
- Are creating a memorable experience.
- Are a true professional.

- Are giving them a choice between two solutions that may be exactly what they need.
- Are prepared to close the account.

### It's Not **IF** They Buy. It's **Which** Recommendation They Will Buy.

The primary reason to have two prepared recommendations is to take the focus away from whether the customer is going to buy and focus on which recommendation they are going to buy! Then, gain agreement and finalize the account!

There will be times when your recommendations are underdeveloped, and you need to back out of the call to re-work your recommendations to fit the needs of the customer. Hopefully, you will have laid a strong foundation for them to be waiting with bated breath for your return. Let me shed some light; most of the time, this is not the case.

### Focus on Finalizing Agreement at the End of the Initial Sales Conversation.

Know this. Once you leave, the momentum, the engagement, the excitement you instill in the customer, is generally not the same when you return. Life gets in the way along with other things that become the priority over your last visit – such as your competition who swoops in the following day and gets the customer to sign.

All the while, you're back at your desk oblivious, working away on the recommendation you could have made. If only you had taken the time to prepare in the first place! Always focus on finalizing agreement at the end of the initial sales conversation. You know this term as the one-call close.

There are (of course) those products, such as in the medical world, where the sale has to be blessed by everyone and their dog. In that case, the gestation period can be over 18 months.

However, in these cases, the salesperson still needs to know their product, who the decision makers are, and how to be prepared with consistent, well thought-out recommendations, in order to make it easy to say "yes." But, for most sales situations, gaining agreement at the end of the first sales conversation works and is appreciated by the client.

## Most Customers Think They Know What They Want Before You Walk in the Door.

It's also a different selling arena today. Most clients have already done their due diligence online; by the time you walk in the door, they think they know what they want. All that's left is the price and who is the best person to buy it from.

This makes it even more important to be prepared with knowledge of your product, what you can learn from the client's website, industry trends, and a few ideas that you can tweak on the spot, once you've learned more during your conversation with them.

### Tips for Creating and Sharing Your Recommendations

**Create an experience for the customer.**

Think about how you can create as real of a situation as possible so your potential client can experience the benefits of your product or service.

For example, when I was selling online yellow pages and direct mail, I would have my art department create an online spec banner from a layout I would submit.

The layout would showcase my customer's logo and include copy that would capture the attention of their customers. I would print out the categories that would be the best fit for them, based on the knowledge I gathered from their website.

Or, if they were an existing customer, based on the categories they were under from the previous year. I then pasted the beautiful, new banner (the artists whom I worked with were amazing) on the printout of their main heading and in the position they would most likely appear.

That way they could see what they would look like amongst their competition. I never guaranteed positioning, because it was first-come first-serve, but my point was clearly made.

I would then print out all other categories where their customers could find them. However, I did not insert the banner there. I wanted them to see their competition and have them realize how much business they were missing by not being positioned there. Yes, I could have done this in front of the customer and on their computer, but here's why I didn't.

**Control Your Demonstration Environment.**

First, at that time, there was no way for them to see the spec art on the live yellow pages website. They would not be able to see their banner amongst their competition. Second, I had no way of knowing how good their Internet connection would be.

Have you ever tried to demonstrate a product on the computer or laptop only to suffer through the donut of death (the spinning circle thing), dropped service, or my favorite, the distracting email pop-up banner?

You want the customer's full attention, and the best way to do that is by controlling the environment. If you demo your products by tablet, iPad, laptop or whatever else is out there, and you are selling an online or marketing product, ask to get a copy of the template that is used when a customer is first on-boarded into your system.

You can create a mock-up of the customer's logo and input some of their personalized data for demonstration, then delete the information and reuse it for the next customer.

I guarantee your efforts will be appreciated because 95% of sales people don't take the time to do this. They rely on their perky personalities and talk the customer to death about the features of their products, only to be befuddled as to why the customer didn't buy.

If you are selling a tangible product such as a machine or widget, think of a way to personalize your recommendation so the customer can see themselves and their team experiencing the benefits of using it in their everyday life.

For example, if you sell copiers or printers, print out copies of the customer's website so they can see the quality of your product and how well it reproduces their own images.

### Create No Less Than TWO Recommendations

Next, create no less than two recommendations that include your base product and add-ons that make sense for the customer, based on what you've learned before your actual meeting. These will be items for negotiation when you get to that point in your sales conversation.

Both recommendations should make sense. The first should be the premium program and the other, a smaller one with fewer add-ons. Both programs should provide great benefits to your customer's needs. I will address more about this later.

That's it! Two recommendations that create an experience for the customer.

Once you have done this a few times, and you learn how to make your recommendations (we'll cover that later), you will:

- Sell bigger programs.
- Increase your sales.
- Improve your productivity. (See more potential clients in a shorter amount of time.)
- Have an arsenal of great customers.
- Have an arsenal of great customers who will refer you, IF you take the time to ask for the referral.
- Win sales awards and company Incentive Trips.
- Capture the attention of management.
- Pave your way to advancement.

Once you have consistently applied the checklist above, to at least ten to fifteen accounts, the process will become organic. Your prep time will shorten because you will know exactly what to do. It is when you are in front of your customers that you will realize how valuable this process is. Your thoroughness will prepare you to handle the curve balls hurled at you by the customer. And, because you are armed, you can provide enlightenment through industry knowledge and stories that your customer appreciates – which leads to a connection and, most importantly, trust. It also positions you for gaining an agreement on the initial sales conversation. This allows you to serve more customers, keep ahead of the competition, and increase your income.

Chapter Three

Don't Sell. Let Them Buy.™

## Summary and Checklist:

**Summary:**

**Think Like a Business Owner.**

- The buck stops with you.
- Take responsibility.
- Hold yourself accountable for providing your customers with a better way of life through your products and services.
- Handle all customer paperwork and digital submissions, ONCE!
- Practice clear and concise communication with other company departments, which will result in accurate, possibly faster fulfillment.

**Talk with the Highest Producing Reps in Your Company.**

- What products and services are they consistently selling?
- How are they selling them?
- Why are they selling them?
- What do they know that you don't?
- What is their approach to account preparation?
- What are the industry stories they've discovered that have opened doors to more sales?
- Whom do they recommend you get to know in the different departments that process your work?
- What is their secret to sales success?

**How to Become an Expert on Your Products and Services.**

**Steps to Learning Your Products and Services:**
**What is the basic product or service that you sell?**
- Learn the purpose of it and understand its benefits.

- What are the different programs you can offer?
- What are the circumstances in which you would offer one over the other?
- What program is right for which customer?
- Learn how to effectively communicate your products, their features, and benefits.
- Know how to quickly locate these products on your rate sheet.

**What are the add-on products? (These are products or services that complement or add value to the basic product.)**
- What is their purpose? Understand their features and benefits.
- When is the right time to add them to a customer's program?
- Who is the right customer for these products and services?
- Learn how to effectively communicate what they are, their features, and benefits.
- Know how to quickly locate these products on your rate sheet.

**Create a checklist, so when you are prepping, you will remember to review all items, in the same order, every time. When new products are introduced:**
- Keep an open mind.
- Believe that management knows what is best.
- If they are a benefit, incorporate them into your account preparation.
- Be the first on your team to sell them, and you'll be seen as a role model.

- If you can't see their benefits to your customers, talk with your manager, marketing rep or another sales rep you respect, to see what you may be missing.

**Sales Success Begins with Thorough Account Preparation.**

**The *Don't Sell. Let Them Buy*, Repetitive Prepping Process Allows You To:**
- Consistently perform thorough account preparation.
- Save time.
- Stay organized.
- Learn what is in your sales arsenal.
- Learn where to locate all-important documents.
- Become a product knowledge expert in your industry.
- Learn the trends in your customer's industry.
- Become confident and prepared.
- Look professional and in control.
- Sell bigger and better programs.
- Increase your productivity.

**Why create two recommendations?**

**You are demonstrating to the customer that you:**
- Gave thought to their business. You did your homework.
- Know how your products can benefit their business.
- Came prepared so as not to waste their time.
- Are creating a memorable experience.
- Are a true professional.
- Are giving them a choice between two solutions that may be exactly what they need.

- Are keeping their focus on "which," not "whether," they are going to buy.
- Are prepared to close the account.

**If you want to:**
- Sell bigger programs.
- Increase your sales.
- Improve your productivity. (See more potential clients in a shorter amount of time.)
- Have an arsenal of great customers.
- Have an arsenal of great customers who will refer you, IF you take the time to ask for the referral.
- Win sales awards and company Incentive Trips.
- Get the attention of management.
- Pave your way to advancement.

**Tips for Creating and Sharing Your Recommendations:**
- Create no less than two recommendations.
- Create an experience for the customer.
- Create a customized demonstration.
- Control your demonstration environment.

Focus on Finalizing Agreement at the end of the initial Sales Conversation.

**Checklist:**

### Account Preparation and Strategy Checklist

**Company and Contact Information Review:**

☐ **Name of company:**
   ____ Note unusual spelling.
   ____ Privately-owned? Franchise?

- ☐ **Address:**
  \_\_\_\_ Territory location.

- ☐ **Name and confirmation of authorizing party:**
  \_\_\_\_ Note unusual spelling.
  \_\_\_\_ Look for signatures on past contracts.
  \_\_\_\_ What is this person's title?
  \_\_\_\_ Are the notes on the account correct?
  \_\_\_\_ Confirm the true decision-maker.

- ☐ **Payment status:**
  \_\_\_\_ Is the account delinquent?
  \_\_\_\_ Speak with the Credit Representative to learn the back story.

- ☐ **Set the Appointment:**
  \_\_\_\_ Who is the decision-maker?
  \_\_\_\_ Who is the person that authorizes _____?
  \_\_\_\_ Who besides yourself is part of this decision and needs to attend our meeting?"

**Account Review:**

- ☐ **Note the present billing:**
  \_\_\_\_ Full billing?
  \_\_\_\_ Adjusted billing for an error?
  \_\_\_\_ Adjusted billing for a customer service issue?

- ☐ **Study the customer's current program:**
  \_\_\_\_ Current products and services.
  \_\_\_\_ Are they up-to-date?
  \_\_\_\_ How long has the customer had these products and services?
  \_\_\_\_ Pull all performance and analysis reports.

Chapter Three

- ☐ **Customer Website Review:**
  \_\_\_\_ Is the website up-to-date?
  \_\_\_\_ What is the customer's story?
  \_\_\_\_ Is the story clear and engaging?
  \_\_\_\_ Is there a "connection" factor?
  \_\_\_\_ Who are their customers?
  \_\_\_\_ Who could be their customers if their message was adjusted?
  \_\_\_\_ What can you learn about the company, its products, and services?
  \_\_\_\_ What are the areas of strength?
  \_\_\_\_ What are the areas of needed improvement?

- ☐ **Click on every tab to:**
  \_\_\_\_ Learn about the customer.
  \_\_\_\_ Learn how your products can serve the customer.
  \_\_\_\_ What is the offer or "ask?"
  \_\_\_\_ Is there one?
  \_\_\_\_ Is it clear and enticing?
  \_\_\_\_ How easy is it for a potential customer to engage with this company?
  \_\_\_\_ Can you talk to a person?
  \_\_\_\_ How easy is it to contact the company (phone number and email address)?
  \_\_\_\_ Are there testimonials?
  \_\_\_\_ How old are they?
  \_\_\_\_ What do they really say about the company?
  \_\_\_\_ Are there blogs?
  \_\_\_\_ What can you learn about the customer?
  \_\_\_\_ What can you learn about their industry trends?

- ☐ **Online Reviews and Ratings:**
    - \_\_\_\_ Yelp.
    - \_\_\_\_ Google.
    - \_\_\_\_ Company Facebook.

- ☐ **Customer Profiles:**
    - \_\_\_\_ LinkedIn.
    - \_\_\_\_ Facebook.

- ☐ **Get to know another side of your customer:**
    - \_\_\_\_ Where did they go to school?
    - \_\_\_\_ How long have they worked for this employer?
    - \_\_\_\_ What are their interests?
    - \_\_\_\_ Look for common ground.

- ☐ **Study Your Customer's Products:**
    List three questions you can ask your customer that will demonstrate you are trying to understand their world. This will lead into how your products can complement or solve issues they may be having.
    1. _____
    2. _____
    3. _____

- ☐ **Study Your Customer's Industry:**
    - \_\_\_\_ Bring new information and insight to the conversation.

- ☐ **Look at:**
    - \_\_\_\_ Blog Posts.
    - \_\_\_\_ Websites.
    - \_\_\_\_ The customer's LinkedIn profile. See who they are following.

Chapter Three

☐ **What are three of the most up-to-date trends in their industry?**

1. _____

2. _____

3. _____

☐ **What story or testimonials can you share that demonstrate how your products help businesses like theirs, stay ahead of the curve?**

_____

_____

_____

_____

[1,2,3] Provide Support, LLC. (2015, February 20). "Shocking Customer Service Facts and Stats (Infographic)." [LinkedIn]. *SlideShare*. Retrieved from **https://www.slideshare.net/ProvideSupport/upload-f118o34o7pif5jgq39reokpfc6219937final**

# Chapter 4

## *Overview of the 9-Step Don't Sell. Let Them Buy, Sales Conversation Process*

*Listen to learn, open your heart to feel, and serve with a passion to help others have a better way of life, and you too will be rewarded.*

*Chiqeeta Jameson*

## Chapter Four

When I began my telephone sales career, every new hire was flown to headquarters for six weeks of intense training, called IST (Initial Sales Training). And, I mean intense. It was a known fact that when a salesperson completed this sales training, they had a strong sales foundation and knew how to sell. In fact, when people left the company, those who had a work history at this corporation were quickly employed at other companies because of their supposedly strong sales training and ability.

The first three weeks covered product knowledge, paperwork, and processing. The fourth and fifth weeks were devoted to preparation, presentation, overcoming objections, and closing. The final week you were in the field with your manager who was trailing your every move. Then, reality hit, and it was up to you to apply what you learned and hopefully become an amazing sales success.

What is your sales training background? Who taught you solid selling skills? Consider the companies you've worked for during your sales career. How much time was spent on sales training? What about on their products and services?

Most companies today expect you to know how to sell when they hire you. The only training you receive is on their products and services. How very sad and shortsighted. Every salesperson needs a check-up now and then to assess how on-track they are. Many times, we get so caught up that we don't even know we have derailed ourselves. Life after Initial Sales Training looked like this. The year was broken into 26 two-week pay periods. Each pay period had its own budget. If you were given a budget of $1000 that meant that you were expected to generate at least $1000 of new or increased revenue from the customers in your territory.

That was ON TOP OF what they were already spending. So, if at the end of Monday (the first day of the pay period), you lost $1000 in revenue because the outcome of the customer visits you had that day either decreased or canceled their advertising, your budget starting that Tuesday just became $2000. In other words, by the end of the two-week pay period, you were expected to replace the money you lost AND find the money to meet your company sales goal by selling to existing or new customers. If you did, then you met the company's minimum level of performance! What if you lost more sales the next day? Ahhh! Overwhelming, right? That was the business life I chose. I accepted it as a way of life. What is yours?

You can't win awards, go on Incentive Trips, or make a lot of money if you only hit the company minimum. Well, guess what? I was a bonehead. For my first few years in telephone sales, my focus was to always hit my company minimum goal. I had blinders on and capped my performance for too long. I usually did hit the goal but so what. You can't move up by only performing at the base level. Remember, I was in telephone sales. Those were the smaller accounts or customers who weren't real yellow page believers. The point is that I was allowing their mindset to determine my mindset.

At that time, I didn't realize that telephone sales were much harder than outside sales. I had the responsibility of handling customers who were advertising because that's what they thought they needed to do, not necessarily because they believed that the yellow pages worked for them. Or, they advertised because their competition had a presence so they certainly didn't want to be left out. For the most part, my customers were not believers in the product. They were toe-stickers. They "tried" it with not much of an investment but expected huge outcomes. Sound familiar?

## Chapter Four

After saying that, I am so grateful that I began in telephone sales. I learned how to read my customers by their tone of voice, their silence, and what they didn't say. My attention to detail in processing their accounts needed to meet a high standard. This was all excellent training for what was to come. I secretly wanted to be an outside sales representative, also known as a premise rep, who handled the really large accounts. Now, these customers were the real believers! But, I was so intimidated by the premise reps and by the amount of revenue they were responsible for. I look back at myself now and can't believe my mindset at that time. I had myself in a box that I created. I didn't realize I was keeping not only myself from success, but I was doing a disservice to my customers.

Then, I decided I wanted more than being a telephone sales rep. I set my sights on becoming a national sales trainer. Right. How in the world could I do that if I was only a minimum producer? Get real! However, my Dad told me all my life that I could be and do anything I set my mind to. I just needed to focus and do what needed to be done to achieve it.

I went to my manager, Karen, and told her that I wanted to be a national sales trainer. I had a teaching background, so I had that part covered. I just needed to become a really good salesperson. She looked at me and said, "It's about time. You're the one holding yourself from reaching your potential. I've believed in you from day one." I burst into tears. I felt relieved that she hadn't given up on me; she believed I had more ability than I saw in myself. I had somehow gotten off track and was not following what I was taught in sales training. We pulled out the training manual. If I was planning on teaching this curriculum, I certainly needed to understand it, be good at it, and increase my productivity with it. Karen had me begin with the very first step –

introducing myself to the customer. She role-played with me. I introduced myself, and then I transitioned to the next step of asking questions until I was blue in the face. This was my focus for a solid three weeks.

I would drive to work role-playing by myself. I role-played until it was organic. I then applied what I learned during my sales day. I got to the point where I knew what to say, even when the customer would begin to go in another direction. How did I do this? I knew where I was going with the sales conversation.

This allowed me to really listen to what the the customer was saying. I adapted and got them back on course. I then learned how to handle brush-offs and got customers to either talk with me then, or set a firm appointment. From there, I did the same thing with each step of the sale.

Guess what? I improved! My confidence was boosted, and my fear turned into determination. Karen also had me add 50% onto my sales goal each pay period. Instead of me barely producing at 100% of my goal, I started to produce between 125 to 140% of my goal.

My goal moved from company minimum to 40% more than was required. I changed my goal and my mindset. I wasn't setting the world on fire, but I was improving. I had finally moved up from the last rung on the ladder. I began winning Canvass Awards and became eligible for the company Incentive Trips. I could now see that I was responsible for my lack of sales.

In my fifth year with the company, I interviewed for the national sales trainer position with Bill, the Director of Sales Training. I was in awe of Bill.

## Chapter Four

He was nationally known for his charisma and speaking ability. After he had offered me the position, I walked out of the building and screamed! I didn't think my colleagues would have appreciated my display of joy. They were always throwing two-column phone books or shooting rubber bands at me over the cubicle walls, which was a sign to lower my voice. I still talk too loudly on the phone. When you talk louder, people can understand you better, right?

I'm Croatian; I'm passionate. What can I say? The company moved me to the southwest where I began a new chapter with new friends and lots of challenges. I also dropped back to the bottom of the ladder. I was the new kid on the block with lots of ideas, energy, and a great work ethic. Bill, my manager, moved on; and, Jerry, the fabulous, moved from one of the training positions into Bill's role as Director of Sales Training.

Jerry could have been a stand-up comedian. He always found the humor in things. He also managed the personality of each of his team members, communicating with us in the manner that we could understand and accept. And, he was forgiving.

On the first day of sales training, we would always show an uplifting, inspirational video to get the class motivated for what was to come. On the last day, we showed a more somber video, a real tear-jerker.

It was my turn to cue up the videos, and yes, on the opening day, I played the wrong video. Many in the class were in tears. I was mortified. Jerry took it in stride, made a few jokes, and got us back on track. Instead of making me feel worse, he just looked at me, smiled, and said, "Bet you won't do that again."

Among my colleagues was an exceptional sales rep, Mike B. Mike's selling ability was consistently between 200 to 300% above quota. He won all of the Incentive Trips and was a great sales trainer. It was Mike who taught me to always follow a consistent format. Never deviate from the path. Never move onto the next step without attaining success in the step before. Even though this was what I was taught when I went through Initial Sales Training, it was Mike who got through to me and the idea finally gelled.

"Never deviate from the path" became a fundamental principle in my *Don't Sell. Let Them Buy, Sales Conversation Process*. Thank you, Mike B. You gave me clarity.

### Where Did The *Don't Sell. Let Them Buy, Sales Conversation Process* Originate?

The 9-Step *Don't Sell. Let Them Buy, Sales Conversation Process* is a compilation of what I was taught in my Initial Sales Training class, what I learned from successful sales mentors, what I read in books from some of the best sales trainers and coaches – such as Brian Tracy, Tom Hopkins, Zig Ziglar, and later Jeffrey Gitomer – and from what I learned from trial and error by falling on my face while in front of the customer. THAT, you don't forget.

I don't believe you can "sell" a customer. I don't believe you can "make a sale." As Bob Burg and John David Mann so eloquently stated in their book, *Go-Givers Sell More:*

> "It's impossible to *make* a sale, because you cannot really *make* other people do what you want them to do.

## Chapter Four

> If you cannot make a sale, then what *can* you do? You can provide the context that allows a sale to happen when the other person makes a purchase. This is not semantics; this is the secret of all great salespeople.
>
> Your job is not to make a sale but to create something else: *value*. In fact, as a sales person you can define your job description in three words: I create *value*."[1]

In the workplace, I believe that value begins with products and services that are of high quality and truly needed. They enhance, improve, solve problems, and lead to a better way of life, in whatever that life may be. If you work for a company that has hit this mark, do a gratitude check-in and consider yourself fortunate.

I believe the mindset of every salesperson should be the customer and what matters most to them. The nine steps in this process are completely devoted to understanding what the customer needs and desires. It is designed to be a comfortable, logical pathway to lead the customer to make their own discovery of success, whatever that may be.

Then comes the structure of the sales conversation. It is designed to keep the salesperson on track even when the customer throws a curve ball. Remember, you don't move to the next step until you have completely covered all your bases from the steps before. I will explain how this is done for each step within the following chapters.

This process is also designed to help salespeople guide their customers to a successful outcome that is right for them, whether it be an actual purchase or not. Unless you are in front of a customer that can't use your products or services, or an unforeseen issue arises, the end result or outcome is generally a successful purchase of your products or services.

Don't Sell. Let Them Buy.™

## The 9-Step *Don't Sell. Let Them Buy,* Sales Conversation Process

### Step 1: Assume the Lead

This is where the stage is set. The tone of the call is established, and important first impressions are made. So, throw your gum away and, whatever you do, don't even think about making a comment about the out-of-date, yellowed family photos on their wall unless you say something nice.

### Step 2: Ask, Listen, Learn

Thought-provoking questions are asked of your customers in order to bring answers to light, which reveal their needs and desires as well as how your products can be of service to them.

It is not your turn to talk, other than to ask questions and maintain a conversation that is all about them. No blah-blah-blahing or let me tell you about my story that can top yours. This conversation is all about your customer, not you.

### Step 3: Summarize

Once you have determined the customer's needs and desires, recap your conversation to confirm, clarify, and assure you are both on the same page. If you're not, the customer will have a chance to put you on the right path, and you will be able to ask questions to ensure your complete understanding.

## Step 4: Educate

Based on what you learned in Step 2, as well as what you learned during your account preparation before the call, share industry and customer stories that directly relate to their needs and desires. Then, share information about your products or services and how they have helped customers in their industry.

## Step 5: Recommendation

Okay. Take a breath. What I'm going to tell you next is the opposite of what you've been taught. There is a perfectly logical reason for what I'm about to say, and I'll address it in Chapter 9, *Step 5: Recommendation*. It works.

Begin by giving the price of your largest program; then, present the larger of the two programs you have prepared. Give the features and benefits using the customer's own words to validate why you are making this recommendation.

Then, give the price of your second recommendation; present it as well as give the features and benefits of this program. Always give the customer a choice. Open your mind, and stop shaking your head. You will have an "Aha" moment when you read Chapter 9, *Step 5: Recommendation*.

## Step 6: Answer Concerns

This is the only point where you want to answer concerns, not at any other time during the sales conversation. (You are going to love Chapter 10, *Step 6: Answer Concerns – How to Handle Objections and Brush-offs*. I'm going to give you so much great information that you will be beside yourself. I will show you how to defer concerns or objections until you are ready to answer them. YOU are in for a treat!)

## Step 7: Gain Agreement and Finalize

In this step, you ask the customer which recommendation they prefer and what other changes they would like to make. You then review the pricing, terms, and all other details.

Sign the agreement, explain what happens next, show gratitude, and graciously leave their office. When you get in your car, you can reward yourself with a new piece of gum, or I would go to Nordstrom to buy a new pair of shoes.

## Step 8: Follow-Through

Most sales people are not good at following through after the sale. But, that's not you. Is it? This involves the processing of the customer's account and all of the touch points – which includes other people who need to do something for the customer's fulfillment.

It's also about all the promises you made to the customer during the sales conversation. Did you take good notes? Where did you put them?

## Step 9: Show Gratitude

Everyone wants to be appreciated. Surprising your customer with a handwritten thank you note a week after they signed a contract with you can go a long way and get you one step closer to getting a referral from them.

Well, are you ready to dive in and learn how to master each of the "9 Steps?" Let's get started. This is going to be fun!

---

[1.] **Burg, B., & Mann, J.D.** (2010). *Go-Givers Sell More.* New York, NY: Penguin Group.

Don't Sell. Let Them Buy.™

## Chapter 5

## Step 1: Assume the Lead

### *How to Set the Stage for the Sales Conversation*

Are you a control freak?

After three years in the training department, it was mandatory that all sales trainers return to the field so new blood could take over.

It was also a fact that, once you had consistently taught sales training, you became an even better sales rep than you were when you first arrived in the training department. Repetition is the main reason. When you teach or do something enough times, the action becomes organic.

It was my time to leave, and I wanted to go into outside sales, or what we referred to as premise sales.

With a teaching degree and five years of telephone sales, I had become a national sales trainer. I was now ready to move into premise sales. But, I derailed myself.

## Chapter Five

Serendipitously, right about that time, the corporation I worked for announced a merger with another behemoth corporation. We were going to replace the entire sales and management workforce for another corporation. A call went out to everyone in the company, anyone who was interested in becoming a manager or representative in premise or telephone sales for this new venture.

I did the dumbest thing. It was as if my spirit and all common sense had left my body. I saw my right hand go up and out of my mouth came, "I'm interested! I want to be a premise sales manager!" A manager? Where did that come from? I had no management experience.

It wasn't a mistake. It was an honest-to-God choice. A stupid, costly choice. I had no one to blame but myself. What was I thinking? All I can say is that I must have been really convincing in my interview because I was hired as a premise manager and moved from the southwest to the east coast. All my expenses were paid. I was even given $10,000 for miscellaneous expenditures. Does this still happen today?

At first, it was like going to Disneyland. It was new and exciting. I had a beautiful new home. I had the title of District Sales Manager and a total of nine newly hired reps in my unit for whom I was responsible, or so I thought. Life was great!

This experience turned out to be the most stressful, frustrating, and costly time in my life. In fact, most of us referred to our time there as being in Viet Nam.

This was not meant to detract, in any way, from our brave soldiers who protected us and fought in that horrible war. It was simply our way of expressing how we felt – like we were in a daily war zone. I certainly learned a lot about myself, but this "choice" is one I would never make again.

There were fun times, of course, and I made great friends. But, I was living on the east coast. That meant, in winter, I would get up at 4:30 AM, drive through icy, freezing cold blackness to get to the office by 6 AM, and not get back home until the darkness of 8 or 8:30 PM. Winter or not, this regimen lasted for almost two and a half years. It was insane!

I was a horrible manager. To this day, I feel sorry for most of the folks who were on my team. At that time, there was not much gray in my world. It was either black or white.

I'm a hot-headed Croatian. And, through that experience, I discovered that I had no patience for those who didn't work as hard as I did or who didn't put in the time to learn the steps of the sale or master their paperwork. Although, I still have a crazy, Midwest work ethic. I will do whatever it takes to get the job done and done right. I also believe, as my folks drilled into me, that you should always do the right thing, for the right reason.

I was a complete control freak. I knew I had to make a change for me and those around me. I missed being responsible for my own territory and accountable to my own customers. I missed being in front of the customers. I loved the product, selling the product, and working with the people producing and selling that product. I was a loyal employee who made a stupid choice, but I was also an employee who learned from that bad choice.

I'm sharing this part of my sales history so you can look at your life, check in with yourself, and see if you are on the path you desire. I also want you to know that, no matter what craziness you may encounter; you are experiencing it because you made a choice with consequences. The question is – how long will it take you to course-correct?

## Chapter Five

After three long years, I finally threw in the towel and asked for a demotion before Bill, my division manager, demoted me. I asked to be transferred to a California division as a premise rep when there was an opening. Bill was a wonderful boss. Yes, I've had two managers named Bill in my career. This "Bill" was hilarious and had the most loving, generous heart. He was also a pushover and a practical joker that we all loved.

Bill was so kind and so patient. He knew I was drowning as a manager. He also said that, for me to be hired as a premise rep, I first had to prove I could do it. Even though my past sales production was good enough that any division would take me, they would only hire me as a telephone sales rep. If I was serious about a premise position, I would need to stay on for a full year and establish credibility as a premise rep. At that point, he would help me find a premise position in California. I also needed to produce at a level that someone would want me on their team. No pressure!

I had white-hot focus and never looked back. When I walked into the office the following Monday as a premise rep, I felt embarrassed that I failed as a manager; but, I also knew that I had given it my best shot. Management was not who I am.

I gathered my wits and asked my sales team for a minute of their time. I apologized for not being the manager they deserved and asked them if they would welcome me as a fellow teammate.

They did, and from that point on, my life in sales took on new meaning. I got myself organized, became a mentor, and became an example for those who were struggling with their sales conversations. I let go. I began to lead instead of control.

Enough of my back story. Let's talk about what it means to "Lead."

Many sales training courses teach salespeople to "Take Control." Do you like to be controlled? Neither do I. Taking control feels forced, cold, and self-serving. The customer is just coming along for the ride and has no say in what follows. Customers are predictable and always do what we say. NOT!

It's all about the mindset you bring to the sales conversation. And, that's the point. Think of this exchange as a conversation. It's a frame of mind that is open, welcoming, and gently "leading," in which the customer is the focus. This is the opposite of a sales presentation that is "rep" focused and "rep" centered.

After you've been shown into the customer's office – you've gotten past the sometimes awkward introduction, made chit chat, and gathered your wits – someone has to begin the sales conversation. And, the best "someone" is you. Why? Because, right off the bat, you want the customer to:

- See you as a business professional who appreciates the opportunity they have given you to meet with them.
- Know you understand their time is valuable.
- Realize that this business meeting has a beginning, middle, and end.
- Feel no pressure to decide to buy a product that may not be right for their business.

**When you "Assume the Lead," you:**

1. Express Gratitude.
2. Acknowledge the Customer's Time.
3. Establish an Agenda.

**Example to Break Down *Step 1: Assume the Lead*:**

**Express Gratitude.**

- "Again, it's so nice to meet you, Craig. I appreciate your willingness to see me."
- "Lisa, I want to let you know how appreciative I am that you agreed to meet with me."
- "Thank you, Mr. Smith, for making time to see me."
- "Nina, thank you for working me into your schedule."
- "Mr. Smith, thank you for agreeing to meet with me."
- "Ms. Smith, I have looked forward to this meeting. Thank you for making it happen."

*Note: If you are in **telephone sales**, expressing gratitude works beautifully for you as well. Just make these minor adjustments.*

- "Hi, Craig, it's so nice to speak with you. I appreciate your willingness to talk with me."
- "Hi Lisa, I want to let you know how appreciative I am that you agreed to speak with me."
- "Thank you, Mr. Smith, for making time to speak with me."
- "Hi, Nina, thank you for working me into your schedule."
- "Mr. Smith, thank you for agreeing to speak with me."
- "Ms. Smith, I have looked forward to this phone call. Thank you for making it happen."

**Acknowledge the Customer's Time.**

- "I know your time is valuable, so in order to make the best use of your time, I'd like to..."

- "It's clear that you have many responsibilities and only so much time in the day, so in order to keep you on schedule, I'd like to ..."
- (My favorite) "I can see you're busier than a one-armed paperhanger, so in order to make the best use of your time, I'd like to...."
- "I know your time is precious, so to be respectful of your time, I would like to...."

**Establish an Agenda.**

- ".... first ask you a few questions to better understand your business and then share information about my (company, products, services). Based on what I discover, I will make a few recommendations for you to consider. After that, you and I can determine if it makes sense to move to the next step. Does this work for you?"
- "...visit with you to better understand your business and the direction you want your company to go in; then, I'll share information about my (company, products, services). Based on what you tell me, I will make a few recommendations for you to review. At that point, if you and I both agree to move to the next step, we can take it from there. Does this work for you?"

**Let's put it all together.**

1. **Express Gratitude.**
    - "Again, Craig, it's so nice to meet you. I appreciate your willingness to see me."

2. **Acknowledge the Customer's Time.**
    - "I know your time is valuable, so in order to make the best use of your time, I'd like to...."

3. **Establish an Agenda.**

- "…. first ask you a few questions to better understand your business and then share information about my (company, products, services). Based on what I discover, I will make a few recommendations for you to consider. After that, you and I can determine if it makes sense to move to the next step. Does this work for you?"

That's it. The beginning of the sales conversation is all about creating a safe, honest environment where both you and the customer can learn from each other. This first step of the *Don't Sell. Let Them Buy, Sales Conversation Process* sets the stage for both you and your customer to be open-minded. It also helps you to focus on giving your customer your full attention.

In the next chapter, *Step 2: Ask, Listen and Learn*, we'll focus on how to engage with the customer, the types of questions to ask, and what to do with the answers.

**Summary:**

**"Assume the Lead"**

1. Express Gratitude.
2. Acknowledge the Customer's Time.
3. Establish an Agenda.

There's nothing more to say. It's that simple.

## Chapter 6

## Step 2: Ask, Listen, Learn

### *How to Engage, Connect, and Understand How to Create Value*

- Learn what to ask.
- Learn to genuinely listen.
- Learn what to do with what you have learned.

Mastering this step will create a solid foundation to develop a strong, positive, and meaningful connection with your customers.

How do you really see your customers? Have you thought about this? Customers are people. They are people just like you, people who have feelings just like you do. They are not inanimate objects that control our paychecks. They love, and they hurt. Most are great moms and dads (or they are trying to be); they make bad decisions, they become distracted, they suffer tragedies, and they care about others – just like you do. You get my drift. Treat them with respect and give them your full attention.

## Chapter Six

Give value and serve them with all that you have so you can help them, and their businesses, thrive. When you do, the universal law of "giving" will reward you. It may not come when you think it should, but it will come when you have earned it and when you are open to receive it. When you do receive, take the time to be grateful and express your gratitude.

During the sales conversation, one of the ways the customer sees value from the salesperson is when they establish an environment of open communication at the beginning of the sales conversation.

This leads to a connection between the customer and the salesperson. This connection leads to trust and to a meaningful sales transaction, which translates into success for the customer and increased sales productivity for the salesperson.

However, most salespeople blow right over this step. They are so excited to talk to their customers, about what *they* know and all about *their* widgets and gadgets that they leave out the most important factor; what the customer wants, needs and is interested in.

I know because I did this for years. When I finally stopped to analyse what I was doing wrong, I was left with one glaring realization – just like what my Dad would tell me when he saw me in a frenzy, "Honey, you're like a fart in a hot skillet. You're all over the place." I am a type "A" personality. What can I say?

This part of my sales call (it certainly wasn't a conversation at that point) was like being in a hot skillet. My questions were all over the place. I would tell myself to focus on my customer and to discover their needs. That was how I was trained. But, I would ask a question, and my mind would race.

I rarely heard the customer's answer, and even if I did, I wouldn't have known what to do with it.

I'm not kidding. I was so focused on what I needed to do next that, over half the time, I wasn't present in the exchange. I certainly wouldn't call that a conversation.

I was winging it in front of my customers. Since I didn't take the time to learn the right questions to ask, understand why I was asking them, or commit them to memory, I found myself asking dumb things. "So, tell me, what is your budget?" OMG! How completely dumb is that? Oh. You regularly ask this question? Well, keep reading, keep an open mind, and see if you feel differently.

It took me forever to learn that nine out of ten customers have no idea what their budget is (or even if they have one). Then, because I asked and they didn't want to look stupid, they pulled some made-up, off-the-wall figure out of the air; a figure which neither of us knew what to do with. We were both stuck. The number was usually too low for me to work with. And, for the customer, it was a "well, this feels good to me" figure. Know this, if a customer wants what you have, they will find the money to buy it.

You do it all the time. You didn't need that new car, but you bought it anyway. You didn't really need that gorgeous $300 purse at Nordstrom, but you rationalized it all the way to the checkout counter.

So, don't put yourself into a corner and box yourself in like I did. Once your customer has declared a budget or figure, your recommendation (if you get that far) will have to be within that boundary.

Why? Because when your recommendation goes beyond that number, you look as if you aren't listening, let alone caring about what they said. And, you are the one who established their budget by asking that stupid question in the first place!

## Chapter Six

If there is an issue with a budget, you don't bring it up. Let the customer do it and defer addressing the budget issue until after you have given your recommendations. Answering customer concerns will be addressed in Chapter 10.

On another note, I may have been a late bloomer when it comes to sales conversation, but I was never heartless. I have always loved helping others have a better way of life. I truly did and will always have the customer's best interests at heart. But, at that time in my sales career, I just didn't know how to conduct a sales conversation. I never thought about my time with the customer as having a conversation, let alone a two-way interaction.

I always thought about it as a one-way street; I was in control, and my responsibility was to convince my customers to buy my products. The sales/customer interaction was always referred to as a "presentation" or "sales call." The focus was on how well the salesperson performed during the call and how much they sold. This is still the case, but it's the mindset of having a conversation over doing a presentation that makes all the difference.

In today's selling environment, most customers have already done their homework, and they either know exactly what they want or have a good idea. If you are granted an audience, you need to discover what they know and if what they know is based on fact. This is critical because it means that your conversation with them begins wherever they are on *their* journey. You need to be aware of the time they have already spent on research, and they may already feel as if they are nearly experts themselves or want you to cut to the chase, which is usually the price.

Don't do it. YOU, not the customer, are the expert about your product. If you truly have the customer's best interests at heart, then guide the sales conversation.

Guide them in an organized progression and in a way that the customer will see the holes in their thinking. This is not about you proving the customer wrong. It's about guiding the customer to come to their own conclusions; for them, there is still more research that needs to be done, or what they assumed was wrong. And, thank God, they had the wherewithal to take a meeting with you! This is the *Don't Sell. Let Them Buy, Sales Conversation Process*. It works, and the customer will thank you for it.

To see how much this landscape has changed, from a short ten to fifteen years ago, think of how a salesperson would have to begin from scratch because the Internet and Social Media were not as reliable for research as they are today. This meant that customers had to rely on what the salespeople told them, what information they could find at trade shows, or what their competitors were doing from colleagues and observations.

At that time, the salesperson had the upper hand because they had all the knowledge of their products and a lot of incorrect knowledge about their competitor's products. This means that when customers were needing to replace or rethink the product they were using or intrigued enough about your product because they had no idea it even existed, they granted you a meeting. Yes, today's selling environment may be different because customers are more informed; but, you know as well as I do that when a decision is about to be made, we all latch onto what "feels" right and what we "think" is the best solution. (Maybe, sometimes it is.) But, when we are not the experts, we tend to pick and choose what fits our needs.

And, sometimes, we draw conclusions without getting all of the facts, and this leads to poor decisions.

All this is to say, my *Don't Sell. Let Them Buy*, belief is that it is your responsibility as the salesperson to take the time to ask the right questions.

It's your responsibility to ensure your customers are aware of all the consequences of whatever decisions they are going to make. Be the professional that you should be, and guide the conversation in an organized progression. The customer will, in the end, thank you for it. More on this a little later.

Moving on, if you're fortunate to go through a top-notch sales training course, you may find yourself in this comfy-cozy sheltered environment for a few weeks. But, once you get on the street, all heck breaks loose, time goes into warp speed, and you're lucky if you remember a fragment of what you learned.

You haven't committed the questions to ask and the order of the sales conversation to organic memory. You haven't made enough mistakes or committed enough failures to have total confidence in what you're doing; so, you find yourself at the mercy of your customers, your sales goal requirement, and your boss. If you bothered to set aside a time to role play with yourself or a buddy, you could hone your skills. But, who wants to take the time to work on their skill set? God forbid you actually learned your trade. Think again.

If you don't stay disciplined, practice what you were taught, and learn how to put the customer and their needs first, once you're out of training you begin to develop bad habits.

In the case of *Step 2: Ask, Listen, Learn* – if you don't "Ask" the right questions, you won't "Listen" to anything but gibberish, and you can't "Learn" how to help your potential customers with your products or services.

When this happens, everything falls apart. You find yourself making a recommendation based on nothing because you didn't discover the needs and desires of the customer.

What's worse is that the customer knows this too! Because you asked the wrong questions, you couldn't gather information to help build a case as to why they need your products. So, why in the world would they buy anything from you? You're a mess! (She says, speaking about her past self and a billion other salespeople.)

Budgets and fears of losing your job overtake your mindset. The "protect my pocketbook" effect takes over your focus, not the needs of your customers. I know this because I lived it. If you feel the same way, just hang in there with me. I'll show you how to turn this craziness into sales success.

If you haven't figured it out, becoming skilled at knowing what questions to ask, how to ask them, and what to do with the answers, is crucial not only to your sales success but the success of your customers. You must master this important skill because every step that follows is built upon the answers you evoke from your customer in *Step 2: Ask, Listen, Learn.*

### What is your mindset?

Do you interrogate, in order to "sell," or do you ask, in order to "serve?"
- Think about it. What <u>do</u> you do?
- What questions do you find yourself asking potential customers?
- Why do you ask those specific questions?
- Are the answers you receive giving you the result you are looking for?

- What <u>are</u> you looking for?
- How receptive are your customers to answering your questions?
- If you were your customer, how receptive would you be to answering your questions?
- How many questions do you ask?
- On a scale of one to ten, "10" being the highest, how thought-provoking are your questions?
- What do you do with the answers?
- At what point do you know when to move on?

Let me ask you again: Do you interrogate, in order to "sell," or do you ask, in order to "serve?"

More importantly, how do your customers feel when you ask them questions? Do they feel they are being maneuvered into a position to be "sold," or do they feel comfortable and safe within an exploratory conversation that could lead to the answer to a nagging problem?

More directly, is your focus on your pocketbook? Are you focusing on a sales goal or on trying to learn not just how but if your products and services are a good fit for your customer? I call this *hollow* versus *fulfilling* selling.

There is absolutely nothing wrong with "selling," in and of itself. We have to be sold things in order to satisfy our needs and desires. It's all about how we are sold that determines the outcome of our sales journey. Nobody wants to buy from a pushy salesperson or from someone who doesn't seem to genuinely care. But, when we're in a sales conversation where we are at the center, and the salesperson seems genuinely interested in us, it's rare, refreshing, and we are more likely to buy.

Let me show you how to become that rare, refreshing salesperson that customers want to buy from. The first step is to understand what you can learn when you ask the RIGHT questions.

**When You Ask the Right Questions, You Guide Your Customer to Reveal:**
- What frame of mind they are in, and whether it's the right time to have this conversation, or if is best to reschedule for a better time.
- Who they are and how best to communicate with them – are they a forward thinker, risk taker, cautious analyser, or fly-by-the-seat-of-their-pants personality?
- How they perceive their business and their company mission.
- What is important to them.
- Whom they serve.
- How they serve their customers.
- What their standard of customer service is.
- What their business does well.
- Why a customer would want to do business with them over one of their competitors.
- What they think of their business as compared to their competitors.
- How they market their business and how well it is working.
- Their business needs or areas of needed improvement.
- What they would change in their business and why.
- How up-to-date they are with industry trends.
- What their goals are.
- What needs to change in their business so they can make their goals a reality.

- How they plan to reach their goals.
- How your products and services can or cannot help them.
- What information you can share with them that can prove value. (This is done in *Step 4: Educate*.)
- What specific program you can offer that will be of most benefit to them.

**Questions to Reveal...**

**Frame of mind:**

There will be times when it is best to stop the sales conversation and reschedule. You can tell when the customer is off or their mind is elsewhere. Generally, you discover this during *Step 1: Assume the Lead*.

- Express Gratitude:

    "Again, Craig, it's so nice to meet you. I appreciate your willingness to see me."

- Acknowledge the Customer's Time

    "I know your time is valuable, so in order to make the best use of your time, I'd like to...."

- Establish an Agenda

    ".... first ask you a few questions to better understand your business and then share information about my (company, products, services). Based on what I discover, I will make a few recommendations for you to consider. After that, you and I can determine if it makes sense to move to the next step. Does this work for you?"

You may get as far as, "...Does this work for you?" before they say, "I'm not interested in anything but the price. What is it?"

**To discover if:**

- This is a bad time to have this sales conversation because something is taking the customer's focus away from your meeting.

- If the customer has done their homework, wants a product like what you are offering, and is focused solely on price.

- If the customer doesn't really know what they want but is price shopping.

You first want to attempt to defer answering the question, because you don't have enough information to give them an answer.

Salespeople with little confidence will immediately whip out their rate sheet, fumble to collect their wits and throw out a rate.

How well does that work for you? Others who tend to be combative say, "A price for what? Based on what?" Don't. Bite your tongue, and take a breath.

Here's a realization that changed my customer and personal interactions. There is no rule that says just because someone asks you question you have to answer it. If you're not ready or if it's not the time to answer a question, defer it and answer it when it's the appropriate time for YOU to answer it.

I will go more in depth about deferring brush-offs and customer concerns in Chapter 10, *Step 6: Answer Concerns – How to Handle Brush-offs and Objections*. For now, here is a highlight of what will be covered.

**Example of Deferring an Answer:**

> **Customer:** "I'm not interested in anything but the price. What is it?"

> **Salesperson:** "I certainly understand that, and I'm going to give you the price as soon as I know what it is. In order to do that, I need to learn more about your business. Then, I'll be able to give you a quote that best fits your needs.

For example, when we made this appointment you mentioned you needed to make some changes. What has occurred in your business that is causing a need to make changes in the way you do things?"

That is a deferral. **A**cknowledge that you heard the customer, **D**efer answering the question, and **P**ush **T**hrough (**ADAPT**). More on that in Chapter 10, *Step 6 – Answer Concerns.*

If the customer doesn't want to move on, then you need to get personal to get their attention.

> **Customer:** "You don't need to know that. Just give me the price."

> **Salesperson:** Take a breath. Look directly at your customer. Be silent for a beat. Then say, "I get the feeling that this is not a good time to have this conversation. Is that right?"

> **Customer:** "Actually, no, it's not. Yesterday, my wife was told she has cancer. Can we reschedule after I get past this?"

>> *Or* "I'm sorry. You're right. I don't have time for this. I have a conference call that just came up, and it was too late to call you to cancel our meeting. I am not going to have time to prepare for it."

Always give the customer the benefit of the doubt. We all have bad days and a life that is always getting in the way of our business.

**Personality Type:**

I am a firm believer that "failure to communicate" falls onto the shoulders of the one who is initiating the communication. If you are trying to explain something and the person to whom you are communicating does not understand, that's your issue not theirs.

It is up to you to discover how to communicate to this person, so they will understand what you are saying. When you accept responsibility for communication you initiate, you will find that your interactions with others will be more successful and meaningful.

There are many books and courses that can teach you about personality types and how to communicate best with each one. The personality type of your customer determines how you should interact with them. I have found that the adaptation of my speech (fast, slow, professional, folksy, direct, reflective, etc.), the information I share to prove value (stories vs. data vs. statistics), and the time I spend with any given customer, directly affects the outcome of my sales conversations.

In other words, pay attention to the personality of your customers and communicate to that person's personality. When you do, you and your customers will have meaningful communication.

The following questions are examples of how to get your customers to really think about their business. They are not for all industries, but you will get the idea as to how to apply them to your field.

These questions are great for those in the field of advertising, marketing, and social media. I have also provided questions for those in real estate and the insurance field.

Notice that all questions are statements or open-ended, which require more than a "yes" or "no." These questions are designed to make the customer think, give the salesperson time to think as the customer answers, and create a safe environment for both the customer and salesperson to learn from each other.

### Ask Direct Questions to Reveal...

Perceptions of Their Business and How Well They Serve:

Lead in: "I've studied your website and the marketing collateral I could find about your business, but I'd like to hear from you directly."

1. **Who is ABC Company and why does it exist? Or, what was it that compelled you to create this business?**
   - How has your company changed over the years?
   - What has caused your company to change?
   - What obstacles has the company gone through to get to where it is now?
   - What obstacles are you facing now?
   - How confident are you that those changes can be successfully made in the future?

2. **If you could divide your business into profit centers, what would they be?**
   - Which area is more profitable?
   - Why?
   - What are you doing to improve the profitability of the other areas?

- Is it working?
- If you could change the direction of your profit centers, how would your business be different?

3. **How well do you feel you serve your customers?**
    - Explain the customer's journey when they purchase from you.
    - What areas need improvement?
    - What is holding you back from making this happen?

4. **Overall, what does your company do very well?**

5. **What is the biggest problem you want to solve in your business?**

6. **What are the areas of needed improvement?**
    - What are you doing to improve? Is it working?
    - What is your goal for making this improvement happen?

7. **If you could change anything about your business, what would it be and why?**

**Perceptions of How Their Business Fits in Within the Marketplace:**

1. **What percentage of the marketplace do you have?**
    - Are you pleased with this position?
    - What is holding you back from owning a higher percentage?
    - What are you doing to improve your position?
    - Is it working? Or, why do you think it's not working?

2. **Why would someone want to do business with your over one of your competitors?**

3. **On a scale of one to ten, "10" being the highest, how would you rank your company against your competition?**

4. **What are the reasons you lose business to a competitor?**

    - What are you doing to stop this from happening?

**Marketing and Industry Trend Validations:**

1. **How happy are you with your website?**

    - What would you like to see changed?

2. **What percentage of business does your website create for you on a monthly/yearly basis?**

    - How do you know?

3. **How else do your potential customers find you?**

    - Is it working?

4. **Where are your competitors advertising?**

    - What is the reason you are not doing that as well?

5. **Where would you like your company to be seen by potential customers?**

    - Why are you not there now?

**Goals:**

1. **Where do you see your business two years from now?**

    - Five years from now?
    - How do you plan to get there?
    - If something were to happen that would stop you from attaining your goals, what would that be?

2. **Is there anything else that you want to share with me?**

3. I'd like to ask you one last question, as your representative, if I offered a solution through my products and services, what would that solution do for your company?

**Do You Ask Thought-Provoking Questions?**

**Real Estate:**

To separate you from other salespeople and your competition, think about asking questions that evoke deeper responses. Take Realtors, for example. Every realtor needs to ask, "So, what are you looking for?" and "How many bedrooms?" I'm suggesting you go beyond these surface level questions.

If you sell residential real estate, you sell homes; but, if that's all you're selling, then you are missing the mark, working a lot harder than you need to be, and leaving money on the table. The business you are really in is emotion, comfort, style, prestige, design, accessibility, safety, peace of mind, security, and so on. Think on a deeper level.

What will separate you from other salespeople is how you make your potential clients feel – the vision you help them create for their new home and the confidence you instill in them for your ability to turn their vision into a reality.

1. Janet, picture yourself a year from now driving into your neighborhood after picking up the girls from school. What do you feel as you drive past your neighbors' homes?
    - What do you see?
    - How big are the lawns?
2. How close are you to the girls' school? A park? A grocery store?

3. Now, what does your new home look like from the outside? Describe it.
4. When you walk in the front door, what do you feel? Why does it make you feel that way?
5. Imagine bringing the groceries into the kitchen and setting them on the counter. Look around and tell me what the kitchen looks like. How does it feel?
6. Jay, when you get up in the morning, and you're headed to the kitchen for coffee, tell me what you feel as you walk through your new home.

- What do you see as you look into the backyard?
- How far is the kitchen from your bedroom?
- Do you walk down a flight of stairs or is this a one-story home?

You get the gist. Think of questions that evoke emotion. You will demonstrate that you are not simply helping them find a new house. You will be seen as a caring professional who understands that this is a major decision; you're taking your time to help them hone in on their unique needs and wants, in order to create one vision that works for the both of them.

They will see you guiding them through the process and helping them find common ground; that way the journey will be easier, and when their dream home presents itself, they will both know it.

They will appreciate the depth in which you are making them think about this huge decision. They will have confidence in you, and you will stand out above the other realtors who are surface dwellers.

## Insurance:

If you are in insurance, you can apply everything I just said to your industry. You are also in the business of peace of mind, security, safety, and confidence. Try the following questions, and you will notice a difference in your customer interactions as well as the number of customers who decide to buy from you.

## Auto:

1. What are the worst-case scenarios you want protection against?
2. Describe your average day, and focus on how much time you spend in the car.
3. What roads do you find yourself driving on the most?
4. Tell me about your weekends. How much time are you and your family are in the car?

## Home Owners:

1. What are the worst-case scenarios you want protection against?
2. Is this your dream home that you plan to stay in or a home that works for you now until your next chapter unfolds?
3. How often do you entertain?
4. What hobbies or interests do you have that involve collecting things that you find precious? Do you display or house these precious items in your home?
5. Has there ever been theft in your neighborhood?
6. Knowing that you have opted against earthquake coverage, if an earthquake were to occur and you lost your home and its contents, what means do you have for replacements?

7. On a scale of one to ten, "10" being the highest, if you were faced with losing everything, how would you rank the importance of having the funds to completely replace what you have lost?

Regardless of what industry you are in, dig deeper and ask questions that make your potential client think. Get them to open up to you about their business. This is where a connection is made, and this is what will separate you from your competition.

**How many questions do you ask?**

To answer that question, you need to think about the features and benefits of your products and services. What are they? List every feature and then all of the matching benefits.

Learn them and, again, make them organic. You never know when a customer's need or want will present itself.

If you are not a product expert in your field, you can miss the opportunity to provide an excellent solution. Don't leave that door open for your competition.

You have already learned what your questions should reveal about your customers and their businesses. However, the bottom line is that no matter what industry you are in, your questions should focus on:

- Connecting, engaging, and getting to know the customer.
- Helping the customer to think on a deeper level about their business.
- Uncovering the customer's needs and wants.
- If those needs and wants can be solved and satisfied by your products and services.

- How your products and services can make a significant change in the customer's business.
- What the customer knows or thinks they know about your products and services.
- The reason why they are just now looking for a solution or what has changed.
- What the customer's future desires are and how they plan to get there.
- Learning how you can be of service through your products and services or what recommendation you can give for someone who can be of service.

So, "How many questions do I ask?" To answer the question more directly, you should have at least eight to ten basic questions that are always, and without fail, your foundation for the sales conversation. Other questions will naturally arise as your conversation progresses.

Your basic questions will keep you on track and ensure that you uncover the necessary information needed to move onto the next step of the sales conversation process.

**How to Genuinely Listen to What Your Customer is Saying:**

The first step is to commit a set of questions to memory that you can ask in the same order, without fail, every time. Yes, you can do this, and it works. I'm giving you gold here. This does work. Doing this keeps you on track and ensures that you receive the information you need in order to make the best recommendation for the customer. You know your products and services, so focus on questions that give you insight into the customer's needs and wants.

## Chapter Six

Make these questions organic. Rehearse them until they become a part of you. That means you can rattle them off like an actor speed-reading their lines. When you know exactly what to ask, you relax, hear and comprehend what the customer is saying. You will also get away from the "order-taker" pitfall because you will be conversational, know where you're going, and will be able to focus on listening to your customer. Imagine that! Once you have this down, the customer can throw you a curve ball, and you'll still know exactly where you are in the conversation as well as how to get right back on track.

The second step, once you begin asking your questions, is to listen, learn and for cryin' out loud take notes. This shows that you are listening and that you care. It also helps you to remember vital information that will be key when you make your recommendations.

Third, when you respond, or you have something to add, think about it before opening your mouth. This is not the time for you to one-up the customer. Let the customer have their day.

You can still have a conversation by asking the customer to elaborate or share something that would be of direct interest – just make it very brief. Steer away from adding your opinion or providing anything about what your products and services can do. This is not the time for that. Stay as neutral and thoughtful as you possibly can while maintaining the order of your questions. The customer will like you for that, because you are giving them the stage.

Before you move onto the next step of the sales conversation, you have to uncover the customer's needs and wants, in order to make a recommendation that makes sense. If you don't, then you can't move on. This should not happen if you have well thought out questions and thoroughly understand the customer's responses. (I've given plenty of examples.) Just sayin.'

Let's be positive. Let's say that you've asked the right questions, you've gathered great information from the customer, and you've got a solid idea of what to offer them. Now, what do you do? That is what we discuss in Chapter 7, *Step 3: Summarize*.

Chapter Six

**Summary:**

Mastering *Step 2: Ask, Listen, Learn* will create a solid foundation to develop a strong, positive, and meaningful connection with your customers.

Customers are people just like you, who have feelings just like you. Give value and serve them will all that you have, and you will be rewarded when it is your time.

Establishing an environment of open communication leads to trust and a meaningful outcome for both you and your customer.

Avoid asking the customer if they have a budget. If the customer wants what you have to offer, they will create a way to afford it.

Even if the customer tells you they have already done their homework, remember that you are the expert about your product or service. Engaging the customer in a conversation will reveal holes in their thinking and provide accurate information for them to make an informed decision.

Ask questions in order to serve your customer.

### When You Ask the Right Questions, You Guide Your Customer to Reveal:

- What frame of mind they are in, whether it's the right time to have this conversation, or if it is best to reschedule for a better time.
- Who they are and how best to communicate with them – are they a forward thinker, risk taker, cautious analyser, or fly-by-the-seat-of-their-pants personality?
- How they perceive their business and their company mission.
- What is important to them.

- Whom they serve.
- How they serve their customers.
- What their standard of customer service is.
- What their business does well.
- Why a customer would want to do business with them over one of their competitors.
- What they think of their business as compared to their competitors.
- How they market their business and how well it is working.
- Their business needs or areas of needed improvement.
- What they would change in their business and why.
- How up-to-date they are with industry trends.
- What their goals are.
- What needs to change in their business so they can make their goals a reality.
- How they plan to reach their goals.
- How your products and services can or cannot help them.
- What information you can share with them that can prove value. (This is done in *Step 4: Educate*.)
- What specific program you can offer that will be of most benefit to them.

### Ask Questions to Reveal a Customer's Frame of Mind to Discover:

- If this is a bad time to have this sales conversation because something is taking the customer's focus away from your meeting.
- If the customer has done their homework, wants a product like what you are offering, and is focused solely on price.

- If the customer doesn't really know what they want but is price shopping.

> A "failure to communicate" falls onto the shoulders of the one who is initiating the communication.

**Ask Direct Questions to Reveal...Perceptions of The Customer's Business and How Well They Serve:**

Lead in: "I've studied your website and the marketing collateral I could find about your business, but I'd like to hear from you directly."

1. **Who is ABC Company and why does it exist? Or, what was it that compelled you to create this business?**
   - How has your company changed over the years?
   - What has caused your company to change?
   - What obstacles has the company gone through to get to where it is now?
   - What obstacles are you facing now?
   - How confident are you that those changes can be successfully made in the future?

2. **If you could divide your business into profit centers, what would they be?**
   - Which area is more profitable?
   - Why?
   - What are you doing to improve the profitability of the other areas?
   - Is it working?
   - If you could change the direction of your profit centers, how would your business be different?

3. **How well do you feel you serve your customers?**
   - Explain the customer's journey when they purchase from you.
   - What areas need improvement?
   - What is holding you back from making this happen?
4. **Overall, what does your company do very well?**
5. **What is the biggest problem you want to solve in your business?**
6. **What are the areas of needed improvement?**
   - What are you doing to improve? Is it working?
   - What is your goal for making this improvement happen?
7. **If you could change anything about your business, what would it be and why?**

**Perceptions of How the Customer's Business Fits in Within the Marketplace:**

1. **What percentage of the marketplace do you have?**
   - Are you pleased with this position?
   - What is holding you back from owning a higher percentage?
   - What are you doing to improve your position?
   - Is it working? Or, why do you think it's not working?
2. **Why would someone want to do business with your over one of your competitors?**
3. **On a scale of one to ten, "10" being the highest, how would you rank your company against your competition?**
4. **What are the reasons you lose business to a competitor?**
   - What are you doing to stop this from happening?

**Marketing and Industry Trend Validations:**

1. **How happy are you with your website?**
   - What would you like to see changed?
2. **What percentage of business does your website create for you on a monthly/yearly basis?**
   - How do you know?
3. **How else do your potential customers find you?**
   - Is it working?
4. **Where are your competitors advertising?**
   - What is the reason you are not doing that as well?
5. **Where would you like your company to be seen by potential customers?**
   - Why are you not there now?

**Goals:**

1. **Where do you see your business two years from now?**
   - Five years from now?
   - How do you plan to get there?
   - If something were to happen that would stop you from attaining your goals, what would that be?
2. **Is there anything else that you want to share with me?**
3. **I'd like to ask you one last question, as your representative, if I offered a solution through my products and services, what would that solution do for your company?**

## Ask Thought-Provoking Questions that Help the Customer To Think On A Deeper Level:

1. Have at least eight to ten basic questions to ask every customer. Memorize each question and make them an organic part to every sales conversation.
2. When the customer answers your questions, listen to what they are saying and what they are not saying. Take notes.
3. This is the time for the customer to talk. Let them shine. Do not try to interject with a one-up story. Before you add something to the conversation, make sure it will be of interest to the customer and will move the conversation forward.

## Chapter 7

## Step 3: Summarize

### *How to Ensure That You and Your Customers Are On the Same Page*

The subtitle of this book states, *Master the Sales Conversation and Guide Your Customers to a Successful Outcome... Every Time.*

At this point in your sales conversation, you know whether your products and services offer a solution for your customer. If they can, move ahead. If not, own up to that fact, and tell the customer why you think your solution is not the right choice to solve their issue or meet their needs.

Thank them for their time and provide the contact information for someone else whom you believe can help them. THIS is an example of "… A Successful Outcome," even if the customer did not buy from you. Why?

The customer's "success" is that they are one step closer to finding the help they need, even if that help doesn't come from you.

You have helped the customer become very clear about what problems they have and what is needed to solve them. You provided clarity. You did GOOD! This is honorable and the right thing to do. And, guess what? This customer will, most likely, remember what you did for them. They will trust you and be willing to refer you to someone who does need your products and services.

You can't win every sale because there are other salespeople who deserve to win too; it may be their turn. Your products and services are not for every customer you get in front of. Even if they are, the timing may be off. That's okay. Accept it. That's life with all of its checks and balances.

Believe this, when you do the right thing for the right reason, you will always be rewarded. It may not be when you think it should or when you are expecting it. But, it will come when you most need it.

Let's say you know you have the right solution for your customer, and it's time to move onto the next step. Let me help you get into the right frame of mind.

My husband and I are built very differently. I am short-waisted with arms and legs from here to Canada, and my husband is long-waisted with shorter, stockier legs. This is an issue when we travel and have one rental car between the two of us. If Craig drove the car last, when I get in the driver's seat, I feel like I'm sitting in a hole. I can barely see over the steering wheel, my knees are up to my nose, and the mirrors are anything but in my line of sight. I end up having to readjust everything to make sure I'm comfortable, safe, and in order before I take off.

As goofy as this must sound, I'll bet you'll remember it. It is an analogy that beautifully explains what you do in *Step 3: Summarize*. Before you move on to *Step 4: Educate*, you first need to prepare and make sure that you have everything in order.

**At the end of *Step 2: Ask, Listen, Learn*, the last two questions I suggested were:**

1. "Is there anything else that you want to share with me?"
2. "I'd like to ask you one last question, as your (insert whatever your industry is) representative – if I offered a solution through my products and services, what would that solution do for your company?"

After this, you move into *Step 3: Summarize*, and you do so with a transition. Try something like this:

"Thank you for being so open (if that is the case). I've certainly learned a lot more about you and your business. Before we move on though, let me make sure that I'm on the same page as you."

Then, you begin to restate the main points that you have learned. Do so USING THE CUSTOMER'S OWN WORDS. This is extremely important because you want to:

1. Make sure the customer remembers what they said.
2. Give the customer a chance to correct wrong information.
3. Let the customer know that they have been heard and understood.
4. Make sure you understood correctly and are indeed on the same page.

If you always ask the same questions, in order, every time, then it will be easy for you to conduct your summary in that same order.

Your sales conversation will have a structure and a purpose, which will keep you on track. Your customer will also have confidence that you are a professional that knows what they're doing. You care about details and getting it right. This creates trust.

**Let's look at the following scenario.**

CRM (Customer Relations Management) XYZ Company Representative has a Sales Conversation with the V.P. of Sales at a company that manufactures hydraulic tools.

> **CRM Rep:** "Thank you for being so open. I've certainly learned a lot more about you and your business. Before we move on though, let me make sure that I'm on the same page as you."

- "This company has been in business for 16 years. You have two locations, one in Southern California and one in Northern California. Now, with the invention of your new *widget,* you're looking to expand into Nevada and Texas over the next two years."

- "You have grown from five to 26 sales reps. When you move into Nevada and Texas, that count will rise to just under 40."

- "Before you move into other territories, you want to create a strong foothold and ensure a strong infrastructure is in place for internal and external communications."

- "You stated that you implemented the ABC CRM platform; it was very expensive, it did not conform to your way of doing business, and it was a nightmare."

Every time someone called the ABC company, they were handed off to a new person, which meant there was no continuity on the ABC side, with your account.

You finally gave up, going back to email and spreadsheets. However, you know that's not the answer. There has to be something better that will conform to how you do business."

- "If a rep leaves the company, the new rep who is taking over that territory has to be given access to the ex-employee's email, spreadsheets, and paper; you said that does not work well especially if the previous rep was not detailed."

- "You also said the company is growing so fast that it's difficult to track accountability and productivity within your sales and customer service teams."

- "The biggest obstacle you have is finding a solution that (1) works and (2) offers something that the president will go for."

- When I asked you, "As your XYZ CRM representative, if I offered the right solution, what would that solution do for your company?" You said, "It would streamline our workflow, provide accountability, and improve productivity."

- "Have I understood correctly?"

    **Customer:** "Sounds like you've nailed it. Now that you know what we need, how much is your system?"

Give the price? It's not time to give the price. You may know what you are going to propose and the price of this proposal, but the customer doesn't know anything about your product. You have not yet proven the value of your product. Give the price now, and they could pass out as a result of the huge price tag being hurled at them out of thin air or throw you out the door.

> **CRM Rep:** "After what you've been through and what you have on your plate, I can understand that you want to cut to the bottom line. Before I do, let's make sure you want what I have to offer." (ADAPT – Acknowledge, defer, and push through.)
>
> **CRM Rep:** "Let me share with you a little about XYZ CRM, who we are, what we are known for, and what makes us the competition."

You have just transitioned into *Step 4: Educate*. And, you have already begun to prove your value as a person who cares. The customer has experienced this as a result of your willingness to:

- Express gratitude.
- Acknowledge their time and busy schedule.
- Provide an agenda.
- Ask thoughtful questions that initiate deeper thinking.
- Listen.
- Focus 100% on them.
- Zero in and confirm their needs and wants.

Now, this is where you begin to prove your value through your products and services, taking the time to educate the customer about features, benefits, and stories that the customer can relate to.

**Summary:**

**When you know you do not have a solution:**

1. Admit it.
2. Tell the customer why.
3. If possible, provide the customer with a reference for someone who may be able to help them.
4. Ask for a referral who may want to hear what you have to offer.

**Transition from** *Step 2: Ask, Listen, Learn* **to** *Step 3: Summarize.*

"Thank you for being so open (if that is the case). I've certainly learned a lot more about you and your business. Before we move on though, let me make sure that I'm on the same page as you."

**Restate the main points by using the customer's words. You want to:**

1. Make sure the customer remembers what they said.
2. Give the customer a chance to correct wrong information.
3. Let the customer know that they have been heard and understood.
4. Make sure you understood correctly and are indeed on the same page.
5. End with, "Have I understood correctly?"

Let's move on to Chapter 8, *Step 4: Educate*. It's time to wow their socks off!

## Chapter 8

## Step 4: Educate

### *How to Prove the Value of Your Products and Services*

This is so exciting! It's YOUR time to take the stage!

Oh, but Chiqeeta, I thought you said that we should be "guiding" the customer and not stealing the limelight. No, I didn't. I said, *Master the Sales Conversation and Guide Your Customers to a Successful Outcome... Every Time.* You've just guided your customer to the point where they:

- Like you.
- Are on the verge of trusting you.
- Are willing to learn about your products and services.
- Are willing to see if what you have will solve their problem.

## Chapter Eight

You've earned the right to take the stage, educate your customer, and prove the value of your products and services. Just remember, do so with the needs of your customer always on your mind and in your heart. Your customer is ready to hear what you have to say. Think about it. They <u>WANT</u> you to have the answer to their problem. That way they can handle the issue and get on with something else. Check it right off that "to-do" list.

However, everything that comes out of your mouth about your company, products or services, and any story or example, should directly relate to solving your customer's problem. Everything should be valuable to your customer.

You know by now whether what you have to offer will help your customer. If it won't, do what I said in Chapter 7 *Step 3: Summarize – How to Insure You Are On a Solid Foundation,* show gratitude for the meeting and for the customer's time. Admit that you do not have the solution for them, and try your best to give a reference for someone who may have the answer. You will have just earned the right to ask for a referral to someone who CAN use what you have to offer.

If you do have the answer, Hot Dog! Then, keep moving, and share your story. Educate your customer.

There is a structure and organization to this step as well. Why? So, you won't forget anything. That way, if you do get off track, you will remember where you left off and how to get right back on. This information needs to become organic too. It is also a "living" step, meaning as your company grows and changes the information you share with the customer will be changing to match that growth.

The beginning fundamentals though will remain the same.

**When you "Educate" your customer, it is important that your information is:**

- Organized so that the customer can easily follow your train of thought.
- Directly related to the problem that the customer needs to solve.
- Relatively brief and to the point.
- Delivered with passion and enthusiasm.

**How to nail this:** identify three separate topics or areas that you can educate your customer on.
- Who is my company?
- What are my products and services, their features, and the benefits they can bring to my customer's business?
- Why would a customer choose to do business with my company over another?

Let's look at each separately.

**Who is my company?**

This is where you begin to build credibility for your company:

- Give a few interesting tidbits about how the company got started.
- When and where the company was founded and by whom.
- Share an interesting story about the company's beginnings.
- Share the company's mission or purpose:
- Has the mission changed? If so, why? If not, why not? Show value and stability in the marketplace.

**What are my products and services, their features, and the benefits?**

## Chapter Eight

When you become the product and service expert, that you know you can be, you will have the customer's ears glued to your every word; because, they want what you have to offer to be the answer to their problems.

But, you must know your products and services. You need to know their strengths and weaknesses. And, truthfully speak to them.

If you don't, the customer buys what you have to offer and something goes wrong because you made a claim that wasn't true; even if you did so innocently, one of those "I-kind-of-sort-of-think-this-is-true-I'll-just-say-it-anyway-statements" will lose the customer's trust in you and your company. Don't do this if you are the slightest bit hesitant or if what you are about to say isn't 100% fact. Flash-forward: think about the consequences and who will suffer if you spew this untruth. Be known for your integrity and honesty. Be known as the product and service expert in your industry.

Every product and service, and their corresponding features and benefits (what you "educate" them on) should do three things:

- Directly relate to solving the customer's needs.

- Enlighten and "wow" the customer with the additional products and services you can offer, which will take their business to a higher level. (These are add-on products that your customer doesn't know exist.)

- Get the customer to see the value of your products and services. Help the customer to envision how much easier and more fulfilling their lives will be if they choose to integrate these products and services into their business.

## Why would a customer choose to do business with my company over another?

Okay. Go for it. This is when you toot your company's horn.

- Share at least two stories or examples that your customer will relate to. Demonstrate the value of your products and services as well as the positive outcomes of customers who chose to do business with your company. (These could be your stories or stories from other company representatives. Just make sure they can be validated!)

- Provide examples of excellent customer service. (Examples that for other companies would be considered going over and above what is expected, but for your company, these examples of excellent customer service are the standard.)

- Provide examples of the advancements that your company is working on. (Make sure only to share the advancements that will most interest your customer.)

With that said, it is important that you deliver this information with:

- Authentic passion and enthusiasm. (Be you.)
- Authority. (You are the expert.)
- Confidence. (When you are an expert, confidence will come naturally.)

## What's the difference between a "feature" and a "benefit," and why is this important?

A "feature" is a fact. A "benefit" is what that fact will do for the customer. The benefit is also the value the feature has to offer to the customer. A "feature" and "benefit" should always work as a team. Do not let any "feature" come out of your mouth without its partner, the "benefit," following close after. Why? Would you ever leave the house with only one shoe? Would you ever drive a car with only one tire? Would you ever brush only one tooth, unless that's all you had? No! The same is true for a feature and a benefit.

Also, if after you state a feature, you ask yourself, "So what?" – Then, you have not provided the benefit. Without the benefit who knows what kind of conclusion the customer will come up with.

**Examples of Features vs. Benefits:**

> **Feature:** "The home I'm going to show you sits on a corner across from the school."
>
> **Benefit:** "You won't have to drive the kids to school. All you'll have to do is walk across the street."
>
> "When you're ready to sell, the fact that you're on a corner will automatically add value to your property."
>
> **Feature:** "Your auto, homeowner and umbrella policies are now bundled together."
>
> **Benefit:** "Bundling all three policies gives you a 10% cost savings."
>
> **Feature:** "Our CRM can record telephone conversations."
>
> **Benefit:** "Recorded calls give you a way to monitor and coach your salespeople."

"When there is a discrepancy in a customer's order, their recorded call can determine what was actually said and resolve a customer/representative dispute."

"If a representative leaves the company, the new rep taking over will be accurately apprised of what was discussed with the previous representative."

**Feature:** "And, you can attach this widget to your belt!"

**Benefit:** "That way you will never have to be without your widget."

"You will never have to bend over to pick up the widget."

"You will be the envy of your colleagues when they see how awesome you look when wearing your widget."

I think you get the point.

**Transitions:**

"Now, you know who we are, what we do, and why we are the competition in our industry. May I share a few recommendations I created for you that will:

> …be the solution you've been looking for?"
> …take your business to the next level?"
> …create new revenue streams for your business?"
> …as you said you wanted earlier, streamline your workflow, provide accountability, and improve productivity?"

If you've followed the prior steps and made a connection with the customer, they will say "yes." That is unless your meeting is running long and they have another appointment, or there is some crisis that has occurred and they need to handle it.

Chapter Eight

They will want to hear what recommendations you created especially for them.

Let's now move on to Chapter 9, *Step: 5 Recommendations* and delight the customer with your solution to their problem using your products and services.

Don't Sell. Let Them Buy.™

**Summary:**

**Your Educational Presentation Needs to be:**
1. Organized so that the customer can easily follow your train of thought.
2. Directly related to the problem that the customer needs to solve.
3. Relatively brief and to the point.
4. Delivered with passion and enthusiasm.

**Create your educational presentation on three topic areas:**
1. Who is my company?
    - Give a few interesting tidbits about how the company got started:
        - When and where the company was founded and by whom.
        - Share an interesting story about the company's beginnings.
    - Share the company's mission or purpose:
        - Has the mission changed? If so, why? If not, why not? Show value and stability in the marketplace.

2. What are my products and services and their features and benefits?
    Features and Benefits Should Do Three Things:
    - Directly relate to solving the customer's needs.
    - Enlighten and "wow" them with the additional (add-on) products and services you can offer that will take their business to a higher level.
    - Get them to envision how much easier and more fulfilling their lives will be if they choose to integrate these products and services into their business.

3. Why would a customer choose to do business with my company over another?

- Share at least two stories or examples that your customer will relate to. Demonstrate the positive outcomes of customers who chose to do business with your company.
- Provide examples of excellent customer service.
- Share some of the company's advancements and goals as they relate to your customer.

**Feature** – A Fact. (The "right" shoe.)

**Benefit** – What the Feature will do for the customer. (The "left" shoe.)

**Never, Ever, Give a Feature without Following that Feature with a Benefit.**

**Deliver Your Educational Presentation with:**
- Authentic passion and enthusiasm.
- Authority.
- Confidence.

**Transitions to *Step 5: Recommendation*:**

"Now, you know who we are, what we do, and why we are the competition in our industry. May I share a few recommendations I created for you that will:
- Be the solution you've been looking for?"
- Take your business to the next level?"
- Create new revenue streams for your business?"
- As you said you wanted earlier, streamline your workflow, provide accountability, and improve productivity?"

## Chapter 9

## Step 5: Recommendation

### *How to Present Your Don't Sell. Let Them Buy, Recommendations*

This is it! You're here! You have the customer's full attention. They want to hear that you have the answer they've been searching for. Or, the answer that they didn't know they needed to hear! AHHHH! This is so exciting!

No dashboard prep for you. You took the time, before this meeting, to prep for this sales conversation, and now you're ready to share your recommendations. And, yes, that's "recommendations." Remember that you need to have no less than two recommendations. You have them ready, and for the most part, the information you learned during *Step 2: Ask, Listen and Learn* is what your recommendations are based on.

Even though the customer hurled a few zingers, these zingers opened your mind to even more ways you can serve your customer.

Because you are now becoming an expert in your products and services, you will be able to add additional products and services into your recommendations – the ones you originally prepared and will now be sharing with your customer during this step of the sales conversation.

At this point, you've just transitioned to *Step 5: Recommendation* by saying something like:

> "Now, you know who we are, what we do, and why we are the competition in our industry. May I share a few recommendations I created for you that will, as you said you wanted earlier, streamline your workflow, provide accountability, and improve productivity?" (I'm using the example where you are the salesperson who is selling a CRM system.)

The customer will say:

> 1. "Sure."
> 2. "Yes."
> 3. "Go for it."
> 4. Or, my favorite, "Sure, but I'm going to grab a cup of coffee first, do you want one?"
> 5. Or, my least favorite, "Sure, but I'm going to grab a cup of coffee first. I'll be right back."

This last statement makes sense if you are in telephone sales. If you are an outside or premise rep, and you're sitting right in front of them, that's another story. Isn't it amazing how many customers don't ask if you would like a cup of coffee or something to drink?

Again, Midwest talking here. Who raised these people? Okay, okay. Don't judge. Just notice. This is their personality. Or, maybe, their M.O. Stay on point, and maintain a "serving" mindset anyway.

Let's look on the positive side of things. They come back with coffee for both of you. They settle into their desk chair, take a sip, look straight at you, and say, "Okay, what have you got for me?"

Now, what do you do? How do you begin to articulate your brilliant ideas, ideas that will solve their problems or take their business to the next level?

If you've noticed, every step of the *Don't Sell. Let Them Buy, Sales Process* has a well thought-out structure; it is a repetitive structure that will keep you organized, confident, and seen as a trusted professional in your industry. The latter will only happen if you consistently follow this structure, commit it to memory, and make it organic. The same is true for *Step 5: Recommendation*. In this step, I follow Aristotle's timeless advice.

"Tell them what you are going to tell them, tell them, then tell them what you told them."[1]

Then, I get the customer involved to determine their thoughts and level of buy-in. I also include stories and examples of other customer experiences and successes that prove value and engage my customer's interest. Remember, everyone loves and learns from an interesting, relevant story. So, to ensure your sales conversations are successful, you need to learn how to tell engaging, true stories as well.

The following is an example of how to deliver your recommendations. This format can apply to any industry, and it applies to telephone as well as outside salespeople. It's straightforward, easy for you and the customer to follow, and it will keep you organized and on track.

For example, you have just transitioned from *Step 4: Educate* to *Step 5: Recommendation*:

> **You:** "Now, you know who we are, what we do, and why we are the competition in our industry. May I share a few recommendations I created for you that will, as you said you wanted earlier, streamline your workflow, provide accountability, and improve productivity?"
>
> **Customer:** "Okay, what have you got for me?"
>
> **Tell Them What You Are Going to Tell Them. (Set the Agenda.)**
>
> **You:** "Based on what I have learned about your business, during my research before this meeting, and what I have learned from you today:
>
> 1. I want to share two (or three, but you must have at least two) recommendations that I believe will streamline your workflow, provide accountability, and improve productivity. (Yes, you are repeating this. These are the customer's needs and their words. Let know you heard them.)
>
> 2. We'll then discuss what works for you and what changes you would like to see.

> 3. And, if together we come up with a great solution that works well for you, we'll discuss how to move forward. Does this make sense?
>
> **Customer:** "Well ....."
>
> **Tell Them. (Share your recommendation.)**

Just as you begin the second phase of Aristotle's rhetorical algorithm, you hear this.

> **Customer:** "Well, just tell me how much this is going to cost."

This is the same person who cuts you off on the freeway. They just have to get in front of you. Let them. Bite your tongue and ADAPT (Acknowledge, Defer, And Push Through). Stay on the path and move on.

> **You:** "I'm getting to that right now. In fact, I'm going to give you the rates, (or pricing. Try to stay away from the word "cost." It brings a negative, cheap association to the solid foundation you have created, and it demeans your products and services.) so you will have them right up front.
>
> This way, as I explain my different proposals, you can focus on the value of each and decide for yourself if the investment makes sense for your business."

Yes, depending on your industry, I am suggesting that you give the price first. You've never heard of doing this? Neither did I until I tried it. No one suggested I do this.

## Chapter Nine

One day, when I was at the recommendation part of the sales conversation, it just made sense to me, and I tried it. I gave the pricing before sharing my recommendations. Yes, I was surprised at what came out of my mouth, and I had a healthy "summer moment." (Guys, that's what you refer to as sweating.)

The customer looked at me like a deer in the headlights. (I will address what I did to lower their blood pressure in a minute.) But, giving the price first was exactly the right thing to do. It worked because I was completely behind the value of my products and services.

The price was not this behemoth thing I was afraid of. It was what it was. I couldn't change it so why hide behind it? Or, as Dad would say, "soft-soap it. "Besides, what's the worst that can happen when you offer the price first? You are not going to lose an arm or a leg. If the customer throws you out of their office, they just did you a favor. Why would you want to work with someone who has that type of personality?

**Remember:**

- You can't "serve" someone who is unreasonable.
- You can't "serve" someone who has no interest in hearing what you have to offer.
- You need to learn when it makes sense to hang in there.
- You need to learn when to walk.

Don't Sell. Let Them Buy.™

I've even been known to tell customers that, for some products, we don't charge enough for their value. Granted, it takes a minute to get used to giving the price first before your recommendations; but, when you look the customer straight in the eye and give the price, you've ripped off the Band-Aid for both of you.

For those of you in telephone sales, it works for you as well. Rather than being able to see your customer, look right into the mirror that you should have on your desk (so you can always "see" what you sound like to your customer); speak with confidence and conviction, and then give the price. There is one step before giving the price. I will get to that in a minute. Giving the price first makes complete sense. Here's why.

Stop and think about what is sitting in the room with you and the customer. It's the elephant, or what I like to call the ominous awning, which hangs over the entire conversation. It's the price that now has your customer's complete focus.

If you don't give the pricing up front, then throughout your entire explanation of your recommendations the customer will be saying to themselves, "This has got to cost an arm and a leg." Or, "Give the price, will ya? Get to the bottom line."

The customer will be so focused on the anticipation of the price that they won't hear your recommendations or why they are the perfect solutions to their issues.

So, acknowledge Kandula (the elephant companion of King Dutugamunu, ruler of Sri Lanka in the second century B.C.) and move him out of the room so that he can relax and graze. Get the price out in the open. The customer may look like they are going to have a heart attack, but stay calm and stand by your pricing.

## Chapter Nine

You must believe your products are worth what the company is charging. If you falter, by admitting they are high or apologize for them, you will certainly lose the sale.

The reaction to hearing the pricing (of most products worth their investment) can be shocking. In fact, they can immediately evoke a negative response. Of course, they do – when there is no context.

So, take a breath, and then provide the context.

**Here is the most important point:**

It is imperative to have the customer's 100% focus. The customer's focus needs to be on:

1. Listening to what you are saying.

2. The value that your products and services can bring to their business.

3. How the customer can be creative and find a way to buy your products and services.

Think of the pricing for your recommendations as a block of ice. Once you give the price to the customer, they may feel like an iceberg slammed down onto their desk. You have the magical chisel (the value of your products and services); begin by chipping away until the customer sees the ice cubes that they can easily handle.

Here's another thought. You don't know what's in this customer's underwear drawer or bank account so stop making assumptions. What if the price you quote is less than the price your competitor gave to your customer yesterday? What if what you're asking is completely acceptable to the customer? You don't know.

So, don't assume. What you do know is the value of your products and services. Be proud of what you have to offer, and provide the context to prove the value of your products and services. Let's continue.

> **You:** "As I said, I have two recommendations to share with you. The first one is the most comprehensive. Grab a pen so you can write this down. The rate for package 1 is $XX,000 monthly..."

Yes, I asked the customer to write, on paper, the rate for package 1 (or whatever your case may be). This is the step I referred to previously; it is done right before you give your pricing. I want the customer to get used to seeing this rate, so if and when they see it come across their desk, on a monthly basis or quarterly basis, it will be familiar and routine. No big deal. Make sense? It sure does.

> **Customer:** "Are you kidding me?"

**ADAPT - *Do not get into a discussion. Keep moving.***

> **You:** "I agree this figure sounds like it was pulled from the air. Especially, when you know you need to make the types of changes we have been discussing, and you're not familiar with the pricing that it takes to make those changes. It's okay. We are going to go step by step.
>
> You told me that the frustration level of your managers and salespeople is off the charts. Just take a breath, and go with me here. Let me show you the value of how much better your business environment can be.

Chapter Nine

> Even if you don't choose this package, you will want to know that it's available to you, and there are parts of it that you will want.
>
> You don't have to take the entire package. After listening to the solutions I have created, you will have what you need to make the best decision for your business.
>
> May I show you what I have created for you?"

Notice that I responded by agreeing. This immediately begins to calm the customer and demonstrates that you are an agreeable person. Never disagree with the customer. There are ways around disagreement. More about that in Chapter 10, *Step 6: Answer Concerns*.

Also, this is not the time to address concerns. There is nothing to base the concern on because you have not given anything to object to…except the price. And, we just covered how to ADAPT so you can get to the context that validates your pricing. Keep moving.

> **Customer:** "I will listen, but I am not going to pay that price."
>
> **You:** "I hear you, and I completely understand. All I ask is that you hear what I have to offer you. I've given a lot of thought, time, and attention to what you and your team must be going through. And, I have divided both recommendations into three sections that address your need to improve productivity, accountability, and workflow. Let's begin with how I can help you drastically improve sales productivity."

Then, go for it.

- Speak with a caring attitude, and take responsibility for educating your customer about your solution and why it is the best solution.
- Remember, this may be foreign to your customer, so stay away from your company lingo or jargon.
- Share your recommendation with total focus on the customer. Be authentically enthusiastic, positive, confident, and act like the industry expert you want to be known as.
- Share the customized spec art or demo that you prepared, based on what you learned from Chapter 3, How to Prepare *Don't Sell. Let Them Buy, Sales Conversations*.
- Your customer will be able to visualize how your products will integrate into their workflow or business.
- Your customer will see the effort you put into prepping for this meeting.
- Once you have stated what your product will do (feature), always follow up with why (benefit) this directly answers the needs of the customer.
- Be sure to address the additional needs or zingers that the customer threw out as well as whatever you discovered but had not prepped for. It may take you a second to determine the best way to incorporate those zingers, and that's okay. The customer sees you working for their benefit.
- Speak in terms of your customer's situation and not a scenario of a fictitious company.
- Help the customer envision and feel how much better their life will be with your products.

- Share how implementing your products will create a positive chain reaction that affects the employees that will be touched by your products.
- Demonstrate how processes will be streamlined.
- Share examples from other customers who had your customer's first reaction and, once they got past that hurdle, why and how their business has improved.
  o Where were they before your products, and where are they now?

**Tell Them What You Told Them. (Summarize.)**

Once you have finished sharing the first recommendation:

- Summarize what you offered.
- Give the benefits, and state why this is the optimum solution for your customer.
- Then, take the customer's blood pressure. (Check in with your customer.)

**Check in with Your Customer.**

>**You:** "Tell me what you think."

Let the customer open up. They will let you know if you hit the mark, need to go back to the drawing board, or are somewhere in between. If you get positive feedback, keep asking questions.

>**Customer:** "I loved most of it, but I can't afford it.
>
>**You:** "Forget the pricing right now. We'll get to that. What did you hear that you like?"
>
>>AND…. "If you were to implement this system, what changes would you like to see so it would completely fit your needs?"

Getting the customer involved in discussing how they would alter your recommendation, in order to better fit their needs, gives the client ownership of your recommendation. When this happens, you know that they are beginning to think of creative ways to buy what you have offered them. And, that's the goal. Help the customer take ownership and see that this is their solution. But, let them have a say in how the solution should be altered so that it will be a perfect fit.

Better yet, when the customer suggests an alternative solution using your products, compliment them and give them praise for coming up with something you hadn't thought of. Giving praise when it is due, while being humble, is never wrong.

You may not even need to share your second recommendation, or Package 2 at all, if the buying signs are there. That, of course, depends on the level of commitment your customer has to your first recommendation. However, depending on your situation, I believe it is very powerful to introduce Package 2 anyway. Why?

- Because the second (less expensive) recommendation, with fewer bells and whistles, will not have all of the fabulous components from Package 1.

- The customer will quickly see this and realize that Package 1 is the one they want.

- You said that you were going to share two recommendations. Unless, the customer tells you they are not interested, keep your word and share Package 2. However, certainly, point out the amenities that are missing from Package 1 and but included in Package 1.

Also, by having a second recommendation, you will be prepared with suggestions and pricing if you need to offer a more conservative option. The point is that both choices provide value to your customer.

Then, this may happen.

> **Customer:** "I really want Package 1. I like everything you said. But, I can't spend that much. What can you do?"

This is a buying signal quietly disguised as a concern. This is good! So, what do you do? You have a choice. You can cave-in and take the focus away from the magic that you created through your recommendation and its delivery; doing so will place the focus all on pricing and the bickering that goes with it. Or, you can help the customer stay in the magic and guide them to make the best decision for their needs – one they will embrace, feel good about, and see a successful outcome from. Which would you rather do?

I used to cave-in. I went right to the rate sheet and began suggesting alternatives. Talk about an order-taker. "If you don't want fries with that burger, how about a side salad? It's a buck cheaper." If you do this, know that there is a better alternative and I will address it in the following two chapters. Stay tuned for

Chapter 10, *Step 6: Answer Concerns – How to Handle Objections and Brush-offs* and Chapter 11, *Step 7: Gain Agreement and Finalize the Conversation – How to Ask the Customer to Buy and Finalize the Sales Conversation.*

I look back on what I did when I first got into sales, and now, I just laugh at myself. But, as George Bernard Shaw once said,

*"Success does not consist in never making mistakes but in never making the same one a second time."*[2]

It's through making ill-informed or poorly though-out choices and mistakes that we learn. That's the path to becoming an expert.

**Summary:**

- If the customer doesn't offer you something to drink, just notice their personality.
- Don't judge and remain in your "serving" mindset.
- Always be ready to share no less than two recommendations.
    - The first one is the most comprehensive.
    - The second gives you and the customer a great alternative if the first recommendation does not work.
- **Follow Aristotle's algorithm:**
    - Tell them what you are going to tell them. (Set the agenda.)
    - Tell them. (Share your recommendation.)
    - Tell them what you told them. (Summarize what you said, focusing on the benefits that provide the solution to your customer's needs.)
- Check in with the customer to determine their level of buy-in to what you are offering. Ask questions to engage the customer, and guide them to take ownership of your recommendation.
    - "What did you hear that you liked?
    - "If you were to implement this system, what changes would you like to see so it would completely fit your needs?"
- Give the rate or price at the beginning and not at the end of your recommendation, because you want the customer's focus to shift from the anticipation of the price to:
    - What you are saying as you make your recommendation.

- The value your products and services can bring to their business.
- How the customer can be creative and find a way to buy your products and services.

- Ask the customer to write, on paper, the dollar amount of your recommendation, so they get used to seeing this dollar figure; it will become familiar and routine.
- The time to answer customer concerns or objections is always after you have given your recommendation, and not before. Until that time there is no basis for discussion, because you have not provided the context on which they can base their concern.
- **ADAPT** – Acknowledge, Defer, And Push Through – If the customer has an issue with the pricing:
  - <u>Acknowledge</u> - "I hear you, and I completely understand."
  - <u>Defer</u> – "All I ask is that you hear what I have to offer you. I've given a lot of thought, time, and attention to what you and your team must be going through. And, I have divided both recommendations into three sections that address your need to improve productivity, accountability, and workflow."
  - <u>And, Push Through</u> – "Let's begin with how I can help you drastically improve sales productivity."

---

[1] **Appleton, D.** (1932). *The Rhetoric of Aristotle: An Expanded Translation with Supplementary Examples for Students of Composition and Public Speaking.* New York, NY: Prentice Hall.

[2] **Shaw, B. (n.d.).** George Bernard Shaw Quotes. *BrainyQuote.* Retrieved from **https://www.brainyquote.com/quotes/quotes/g/georgebern121841.html**

Don't Sell. Let Them Buy.™

## Chapter 10

## Step 6: Answer Concerns

### *How to Handle Objections and Brush-Offs*

You have just shared your brilliant recommendations with your customer. You checked in with the customer to hear their feedback and got them involved in a conversation, in which you discussed how they would alter your premium recommendation to fit their needs better. They are beginning to take ownership of your main recommendation. You feel great! You have proven value, and the customer seems to like what you have to offer. Then, this happens.

> **Customer:** "I really want your first proposal if you cut the price in half."

What? Are they for real? There is no way that can happen! Now your blood pressure just dropped, and you're about to fall off your chair. Take a breath and look at the situation.

This is good! The customer wants what you have to offer. (At least, they are telling you they want it. You need to find out their level of interest.)

## Chapter Ten

This is bad because you can't cut the price in half. It is possible that the customer really wants to accept your proposal but can't afford to buy what you're offering. So, you need to ask questions and rework your proposal keeping the customer involved.

However, what if somewhere along the line you did not prove the value of your products and services? At least, that is your immediate reaction when the customer asked you to cut the rate in half.

Just wait a minute. Get your wits in order. Did you, in fact, prove the value? Or, is this is a smokescreen the customer has created to test you and see if you will come down in price? Which is it?

What you say next will determine the outcome and, more importantly, your customer's outcome from this sales conversation.

**Let's take a step back to learn:**

- What are the five reasons customers "say" they won't buy from you?
- Why do customers buy from you instead of your competitor?
- What is a customer Objection versus a Brush-Off?
- How do you defer a customer objection until you are ready to answer it?
- Why are you, the salesperson, responsible for creating customer objections?
- What is the strategy to overcome customer Objections and Brush-Offs?

**What are the five reasons customers say they won't buy from you?**

Assuming that your products and services offer viable solutions for your customer, there are five basic reasons your customer may voice an Objection. These reasons are as valid today as they were when Zig Ziglar, American author, salesman and motivational speaker, penned them. I challenge you to come up with an Objection or Brush-Off that doesn't fit into one of these basic categories.

1. No Need – "We're happy with what we're doing now."
2. No Money – "That costs too much."
3. No Hurry – "Call me in a few months."
4. No Trust (I like to refer to this as "Confidence.") – "We've tried something like this before, and it didn't work."
5. No Desire – "Implementing your system into our workflow is too much of a disruption."

As a salesperson, you need to learn how to discern if the objection being stated is, in fact, the real issue or if it's a smokescreen for another issue. I will address this shortly.

**Why do customers buy from you instead of your competition?**

I find buying tires for my car utterly boring. I know I need them, but where's the fun in buying tires? I would much rather buy an original watercolor painting, so every time I look at it, it takes me to a place of beauty and serenity. What is the difference between these viewpoints?

There is no emotional pull when I talk about buying tires. However, when I talk about my willingness to spend money on an original painting that makes me feel relaxed and brings me joy, you can see how this is my preferred choice. Purchases may be "logical." We may "need" to buy things, but until emotion comes into play, we tend to put off the act of buying that "logical" thing we need or should buy.

Chapter Ten

Let me add emotion into the tire buying scenario. My husband needs to take my car on a business trip to San Diego because his car will be in the shop during the time he's away. When he asks me if he can take my car, it is then that emotion takes over; I make a beeline to the tire dealer to have all four tires replaced.

Why? Because I'm fearful of my precious husband hydroplaning on the freeway during a downpour. (Yeah, like it rains in California, but you get my point)

Believing that my husband will run into another car, because I didn't replace the tires before he left for his trip, became the emotional catalyst I needed to make that purchase. I would have eventually purchased the tires, but it was the emotional push that lead me to buy them sooner rather than later.

In your case, as a salesperson, if you and your competitor's products and services were equal, why a customer buys from you is fundamentally based on EMOTION.

- How much the customer likes you over your competitor.
- How much the customer trusts you over your competitor.
- How much better you make the customer feel about their buying decision over what your competitor makes the customer feel.

We buy things based on emotion. We begin to buy things based on logic, but it's when emotion enters the mix that the final decision about the purchase is determined.

**What is a customer Objection versus a Brush-Off?**

## Objection:

To keep a positive frame of mind, choose to think of an Objection as active resistance voiced by the customer. They want you to prove them wrong and show them how to move forward with your solution successfully.

## Example Objections include:

- "That costs too much." (No Money)
- "I've got a system that works just fine." (No Need)
- "Give me a call next year. Maybe I will be ready to hear about it then." (No Hurry)
- "We've tried something like this before, and it didn't work." (No Confidence)
- "Your product is new on the market. I don't trust it." (No Confidence)
- "I haven't heard good things about your support system." (No Confidence)
- "I'm not convinced you can handle the volume we generate." (No Confidence)
- "Implementing your system into our workflow is too much of a disruption." (No Desire)

And, the list goes on.

An important point to keep in mind is always to be truthful about what your products and services can do.

Never lead your customers to believe that your products and services can do more than what they can do. In the heat of the moment, the less confident salespeople will find themselves overcoming an objection by zealously promising to deliver what can't be delivered.

The aftermath is not pretty. In the eyes of the customer, the salesperson will lose their reputation along with their company's reputation.

**An Objection is:**

1. **As seen by poor to average salespeople:**

    - A stumbling block that normally has a negative outcome.
    - An indication that the customer is not listening to what the salesperson is saying.

2. **As seen by successful to superstar salespeople:**

    - A signal.
        - A buying sign that the salesperson and the customer are on common ground.
        - An indication that the salesperson and customer are not on common ground.
    - An indication that the salesperson has yet to prove the value of their products and services in a way that resonates with the customer.
    - A real concern that requires the salesperson to authentically communicate empathy and understanding; an opportunity to guide the customer to embrace an unfamiliar way of thinking and offer a new solution to the customer's source of dis-ease.
    - A smokescreen that is hiding the real concern.

Notice that a poor to average salesperson lays blame on the customer for not accepting the salesperson's solution. This is the main reason why these salespeople are low producers. While the successful to superstar producers assume the responsibility for the entire sales conversation, they are also focused on how to communicate effectively to provide clarity and understanding for their customer. The high producing to superstar salespeople take ownership.

**Smokescreens:**

Smokescreens happen when the customer doesn't want to admit their real Objection or concern, whether it is their desire to be polite to you, conceal something from you or their own embarrassment.

Know that it is up to you to listen between the lines in order to discern if the Objection that is (or is not) being voiced by the customer is, in fact, their real concern. The only way for you to determine that is by asking questions.

I want to point out that if the customer is putting up a smokescreen and you don't unmask it, then the entire meeting could go south very quickly. It's not what the customer tells you; it's what they are NOT telling you.

### Unspoken Objection: No Desire – Smokescreen of politeness masking a desire not to have the meeting.

For example, at the very beginning of the sales conversation, it's important to be keenly aware of the customer's frame of mind. They won't or can't buy from you if their mind is not on having a meaningful engagement with you. If you notice that this is the case, try this.

> **You:** "John, is something bothering you? Would it be better if we rescheduled our meeting to perhaps Thursday or Friday?"

> **John:** "I'm sorry. I have a customer whose shipment never arrived. I need to find out where it is and get back to them. Would you mind rescheduling?"

Most of the time, when you call out a situation like this, the customer will appreciate your kindness and genuine focus on their needs. This goes a long way to build trust and rapport. You also kept the both of you from wasting each other's time.

I will address examples of other smokescreens later in this chapter.

**Brush-Off:**

A Brush-Off is usually voiced when you are trying to get an appointment, during your conversation either on the phone or in a follow-up meeting, and after you've had your initial sales conversation. Generally, Brush-Offs happen after you have made your recommendation. If they do, know that you have not made as deep of a connection with your customer as you may have thought. Think of a Brush-Off as a smokescreen that is hiding the real issue.

**Examples of "Brush-Offs" include:**

- "I need more time to think about it."
- "I will include your proposal when we discuss next year's budget."
- "I'm too busy right now to think about this."
- "I'll talk it over with my partner."
- "We're happy with what we're doing now."
- "Call me in a few months."
- "I need to check with the board." (My favorite is when the customer is a one-person show, and you both know it.)

The way to overcome a Brush-Off is the same as overcoming an Objection. This will be addressed at the same time later on in this chapter.

**How do you defer a customer Objection until you are ready to answer it?**

The time to address a customer Objection is after you have made your recommendations and had a meaningful discussion about them with your customer – not before this point in the sales conversation.

Oh, but, Chiqeeta, what do I do if the customer is pushing me for the price?

A price for what? Based on what?

Think about this. If you give the price of your recommendation before you've had the chance to:

- Make a connection with the customer...
- Ensure that the customer is in the right frame of mind for your meeting...
- Ask questions to uncover the needs and wants that validate your recommendation is right for your customer...

Then, you will be shooting both you and your customer in the proverbial foot.

But, you say, the customer has already done their homework. They know what they need and want. All they are looking for is the price. Really?

**Let me ask you the following questions:**

1. What research did the customer do?

## Chapter Ten

2. Who did it? The customer or did someone else do it and give it to the customer?
3. What does this research look like?
4. What does the customer know about your products and services?
5. What does the customer know about the competitor's products and services?
6. What if the customer is comparing lamp shades to skateboards?
7. Is the customer favoring your competitor, because as of yet, they don't know you from a hole in the wall?
8. Did the competitor roll over and give the price or stand their ground and have a heart-to-heart conversation with the customer?
9. If they did, and you gave the price without standing your ground and having a heart-to-heart conversation with the customer, what impression do you think you made on the customer?
10. What type of wood do you prefer I use to hit you on the head to knock some sense into you?

It doesn't matter if the customer said they have "already done their homework." Unless you know the customer's definition of "homework" is completely aligned with your products and services, benefits and value points, you don't have enough information to warrant giving the customer any price. If you do give "the price," and the customer buys from you, that's not representative of being a successful salesperson; that's just dumb luck. I guarantee you will rarely make the sale when you give "the price." This is like throwing darts in the dark. Do it, and you may hit their dog!

If the customer does buy, the sale is founded on price alone. You have no connection with the customer. And, the customer has a limited idea of the value of what your products can do for them. This is a hollow relationship that can go sideways at any moment.

Then, you say, but they said they don't have time to sit down with me and get into a long, drawn out discussion. Seriously? Are you telling me that those C-level managers, mid-level managers, and purchasing agents, who are responsible for buying large ticket items are willing to get half (or less) of the critical information needed to make a decision that could potentially put them out of business?

Then, you tell me, but Chiqeeta, they told me they have already done their homework and know they want the product I have to offer but they are basing their decision on price and trying to decide whom to buy it from.

Okay. Get a grip on yourself. Think about this. How long did it take you to learn about your products and services? What they do well? What their idiosyncrasies are? How about the turn-around time, processing and on and on? Are you telling me this potential customer knows this and they aren't even employed at your company? How and when did they learn this information or from whom?

Let's throw in the servicing of this account. If this company is basing their entire decision on price, how do you know if this customer is the right fit for you and your company? You know nothing about this customer except that they may buy from you! They could be your worst nightmare disguised as a big fat $ sign!

Know this. In order for 95% of all meaningful sales to stick, there needs to be a foundation of knowledge (based on reality), value (realized by the customer), and a relationship based on trust (between the salesperson and the client).

The customer may say they don't have time to sit down with you, but is giving the price (of anything) without context the right thing to do for the customer? For you? For your company?

Customers do not know what's best. Where they, and you, get into trouble is when you allow them to plod along as if they do know what's best.

YOU are a professional, so assume that role. Honor yourself, your company, its products and services, and your customers by treating all communication between you and your customers with respect. Respect, when in front of your customer, is shown by:

- How you carry yourself.
- How you dress.
- How you groom yourself.
- How you talk about your:
    o Company.
    o Products and services.
    o Pricing.
    o Yourself.
- How you talk about your competition.
- How much of the sales conversation is focused on the customer.
- How you conduct yourself during every conversation with the customer.
- Your follow-through.
- Your demonstration of gratitude.

Your end goal is to create a successful outcome for your customers. To do this, you must have meaningful, accurate communication with your customers in order to know if you have the right solution for what they need and they understand what they are getting when they buy what you have to offer. You can't do this if customers won't talk to you. It is your job to change their thinking, and get them to talk to you. So, get them to talk to you!

Understand that the customer sees hundreds of salespeople every year. Most are substandard at best. Choose to stand out and above the fray of mediocre salespeople. Be a breath of fresh air for your customers. Help them enjoy your phone and sales conversations. When you have respect for who you are, what you do and how you do it, you create respect for yourself in others. Demand this of yourself.

One of the most effective statements I say to customers, who are short with me, rude or want me to "cut to the bottom-line," is this. Me: "Have I said something to upset you?" Or, "Did something happen, before we sat down, that has upset you?"

I can't tell you how many times, after asking one of these questions, I stopped the customer dead in their tracks. They realized that whatever they were carrying around with them was ending up in my face. I hit them with a reality check, a respectful but verbal slap nonetheless, and they apologized. They also realized that I'm a person just like them that feels as deeply as they do.

On the other hand, there are those characters who are jerks. That's who they are. Stand your ground by always being respectful, and serve as best you can, as much as they will allow you to do. But, as I stated before, you also need to learn when to walk away.

## Chapter Ten

**ADAPT:**

To help me remember the steps to defer, I created the acronym of **ADAPT**.

- **A** – Acknowledge
- **D** – Defer
- **A** – And
- **P** – Push
- **T** – Through

Let me demonstrate how to **ADAPT** or defer the question of price when the customer has not scheduled enough time to meet with you.

**Customer:** "I don't have a lot of time. Would you just give me the price of your Wachet system, including five Prongs and two Divets?"

**You:** "Oh, how much time can you give me?"

**Customer:** "I've got another meeting in about 15 minutes."

**You: (Acknowledge)** "Oh, so you really are in a rush."

**(Defer)** "Why don't we reschedule for either this time tomorrow morning or Thursday morning? Will either of those times work for you?"

**Customer:** "Would you just give me the price?"

**You: (Defer):** "I will certainly give you the pricing; however, just as you are an expert in your business, I'm the industry expert in mine. I have too much respect for what you are trying to do here not to take the time to better understand your business.

The Wachet is constantly going through upgrades. I may have something that will better fit your needs and may be less expensive.

**(And, Push Through)** "For both of us to discover this so that you can make the best-informed decision, would you make time for me to come back either tomorrow or Thursday? In fact, I'd be happy to bring your favorite specialty drink from Starbucks."

**Customer:** "Okay, but I have to stay within my budget. Come in tomorrow. Same time. I'll give you an hour."

**You:** "Great. And, just know, I have your best interests at heart. Now, what beverage is your preference?"

Notice, I didn't ask the amount of the customer's budget. I don't want to know. As I stated in an earlier chapter, let the customer put themselves in a box. Don't be responsible for doing it for them. There may not be a budget. Remember, if someone wants something bad enough, they will find a way to get it. Unless the customer states the budget, leave it alone.

Now, let me demonstrate how to get into a meaningful conversation with the customer and defer the question of price until you are ready to discuss it. In this instance, the customer has scheduled a time to meet with you.

You just came off of *Step 1: Assume the Lead.*

**You:**

**Express Gratitude:** "Again, Juliann, it's so nice to meet you. I appreciate your willingness to see me."

**Acknowledge the Customer's Time:** "I know your time is valuable, so in order to make the best use of your time, I'd like to...."

**Establish an Agenda:** ".... first ask you a few questions to better understand your business and then share information about my (company, products, services). Based on what I discover, I will make a few recommendations for you to consider. After that, you and I can determine if it makes sense to move to the next step. Does this work for you?"

**Customer:** "I'm not interested in anything but the price. What is it?"

**You: (Acknowledge)** "I certainly understand that, and I'm going to give you the price as soon as I know what it is.

**(Defer)** In order to do that, I need to learn more about your business. Then, I'll be able to give you a quote that best fits your needs. For example, when we made this appointment, you mentioned you needed to make some changes. It's possible that those changes may have an effect on which of my products are right for your situation.

**(And, Push Through)** What has occurred in your business that is causing a need to make changes in the way you do things?"

And, keep moving.

Remember, follow the structure of the *Don't Sell. Let Them Buy, Sales Conversation Process.* This gives you the confidence to be the professional the customer wants on their team.

**Why are you, the salesperson, responsible for creating customer objections?**

1. **You failed to ask the right questions to uncover the customer's needs and wants.**

   Chapter 6, *Step: 2: Ask, Listen, and Learn*, discusses the importance of creating and asking questions that uncover a customer's needs and wants. However, it is just as important that those questions are thought-provoking so the customer thinks on a deeper level.

   This gets the customer to realize they have these needs and wants. And, when you get the customer to articulate those needs and wants, a meaningful conversation builds a strong footing for your recommendation. If you fail to do this, then your recommendation will be based on what? The idea that you "think" your products and services are right for your customer? What about the customer? How can you draw this conclusion if you don't guide the customer through a conversation with well thought-out questions, whose answers may or may not substantiate your recommendation?

   When you fail to ask the right questions in order to uncover a customer's needs and wants, you invite customer objections throughout the sales conversation. To avoid this, ask thought-provoking questions that uncover a customer's needs and wants, and ensure that the customer realizes their needs and wants as well.

2. **You have not asked questions to uncover needs and wants in the right way.**

Ask open-ended questions that compel the customer to think about what you said and open up to share their thoughts. These are questions that begin with what, why and how. Listen to the answers and continue to ask open-ended questions. Doing so will give you the ammunition to use when they may later present you with any objections. This is gold! It will be the customer's words that you use to answer their objections. If you can't get the customer to open up, you will have no foundation on which to build the case for your recommendations or your answers to their objections. Remember, the objective is to guide the customer, not force-feed them.

3. **You have not proven the value of your products and services.**

   Chapter 8, *Step 4: Educate – How to Prove the Value of Your Products and Services,* discusses exactly what the title states. Proving value should be your goal throughout the entire sales conversation. You need to ask the right questions to uncover the customer's needs and wants; and, also address those needs and wants by clearly communicating to your customer what you have to offer and why your products and services are the best solutions with the best value.

4. **You have not connected with the customer nor established their trust in you as a salesperson.**

   There are always personality differences and conflicts. There are just some customers who won't click with you for whatever reason. However, it is your responsibility to give it your best shot.

The way you give it your all is by having a continued smile on your face (even when on the phone), a positive can-do attitude, expert product knowledge of your products and services, and a friendly, non-combative personality that rolls with the punches. Is this you?

I admit that I have a short fuse and have had to bite my tongue more times than I can count. But, my customers know that I will always speak the truth, suggest only solutions that have their best interests at heart, and go to the wall for them to right a wrong that may have occurred concerning my products or services. Can you say the same?

5. **You hold the pricing of your recommendation until after you give your recommendation.**

   Keep the customer's focus on the benefits of your products and services as well as what value they will bring to the customer's business.

   As I grew as an industry expert in my field, so did the size of my recommendations. Why? Because I saw how I could positively impact the lives of my customers through my products and services. When they prospered, this gave me confidence; it made my heart sing to know I was bringing real value to the table and for all concerned.

   By giving the pricing before I shared my recommendation and asking the customer to write that figure on paper, so they could see it while I gave my recommendation, was a game-changer for both my customer and me.

## Chapter Ten

That iceberg of a dollar figure may have obscured my customer's view; but, I used my chisel, comprised of a customized demo, examples of success stories, and value-packed explanation, to carve that iceberg of gloom into a formation of success that the customer could see and embrace.

**What is the strategy to overcome customer Objections and Brush-Offs?**

Having a strategy will allow you to guide the customer to overcome their own Objection or Brush-Off.

1. **Listen, Listen, Listen.**

    The customer just gave you an Objection. Listen to hear what they are really saying. Are you hearing the real Objection, a smokescreen, or is the customer partially thinking out loud? For example:

    Customer: "I don't think this is for my business." (Objection: No Need, or is it something else?)

2. **Use Silence.**

    Take a breath; look directly at the customer. Let them see you are thinking about what they just said and be silent.

    Silence, when used wisely, is an amazing tool. Use silence, after an objection is voiced, as a way to stabilize and center the conversation. Silence gives you both a chance to zero in on what was just articulated.

    Then, comes clarity. This can come from you or your customer. Remember, you can interpret what the customer said completely different than what they meant. Hold your horses and see if clarity comes from the customer. For example:

**Customer:** "I don't think this is for my business."

(Silence. The customer sees you take in what they just said.)

**Customer:** "I mean the part of your recommendation that records all the calls. We don't need that part."

You just discovered that the customer is not objecting to your recommendation - just a piece of it. They are mulling over your recommendation, part by part. They are imagining what the implementation of your CRM system would be like on a daily basis. If you had immediately responded, you would seem more interested in pushing your system than guiding your customer to make the best-informed decision.

3. **Ask Questions to Draw the Customer Deeper Into their Objection or Brush-Off.**

   There is no rule that says when someone asks you a question or presents you with a statement that you must immediately answer it. Knowing this is THE key to overcoming an Objection and Brush-Off.

   **The reasons for asking questions after an Objection or Brush-Off is to:**

   1. Get the customer to think about what they have just said.
   2. Understand if the objection is real or a smokescreen.

## Chapter Ten

3. Buy you time to gather your thoughts as to what direction you need to take in the sales conversation.

Let's look at this scenario.

> **Customer:** "I don't think this is for my business."
>
> (Silence. The customer sees you take in what they just said. The customer says nothing more.)
>
> **You:** "Tell me more."
>
> (That's it. Don't say anything else. This forces the customer to explain what they mean.)
>
> **Customer:** "I really like how easy your system is to navigate (buying sign), but I want a simpler system without all of the bells and whistles. This just won't work for our situation."

Is your customer objecting to the features of your product or are they objecting to the price? Keep questioning to guide the customer for clarity, and get to the root of what they are trying to tell you and themselves.

Your goal is to get the customer to reveal the real Objection, so it is on the table in front of both of you. Do this by focusing on what they like about your product.

> **You:** "So I have a better understanding, what have I shown you that would improve productivity and you can see your people using on a daily basis?"
>
> **Customer:** "All of it, but I can't pay what you're asking."

AHA! Price is the issue! That elephant just came back in the room. Move it out, and keep guiding your customer.

> **You:** "I understand. Let's put price in the corner. Let's forget it for now and focus on what you like and what you need. At the beginning of our conversation, you stated that you need a system that will increase your team's productivity and accountability. You gave me all the reasons why the system you have now doesn't do this. You paid a lot of money for it and are not happy. Right?"

This is the ammunition (the customer's words) you gathered from *Step 2: Ask, Listen, Learn*, at the beginning of your sales conversation.

> **Customer:** "Yes, and I am not going down that path again."
>
> **You:** "Understood. Let's review the features and benefits of this recommendation; and, you tell me which ones if you had your people working with today, would improve their productivity and accountability. Why would they be an improvement over what you are doing?"
>
> Do you get the idea?

If you haven't discovered it already, the *Don't Sell. Let Them Buy, Sales Conversation Process* is designed so that, by the time you make your recommendation, the only Objection that should come up is price. Why? Because, if you followed this process, you will have done an outstanding job:

- Preparing two thorough and customized recommendations to share with the customer.
- Showing gratitude and then engaging and connecting with your customer.

- Asking the right questions in the right way that uncovers the customer's needs and wants.
- Guiding the customer so they realize what they need and want.
- Deferring all Objections until after you have made your recommendations.
- Educating your customer about your products and services through:
    - A customized demo that highlights the features and benefits of your products and services that would most interest your customer.
    - Engaging customer stories in which your customer can relate to.
- **Sharing your recommendations:**
    - By first giving the price and having the customer write it on paper so the elephant can be moved out of the room. Then proceed to use your verbal chisel and chip away at the iceberg of "price."
    - With your customer in an authentic, passionate way that is uniquely you.
    - In an organized, convincing way, so objections about your products, features, and benefits vanish before the customer thinks of them.
- Guiding the customer to become involved and invested in your recommendations.

By this point in the sales conversation, if price is the last Objection remaining and the customer wants what you have to offer, and unless they truly can't afford or create a way to afford what you're offering, you and the customer are most likely in a great position.

Here are powerful questions for you to ask when the Objections are based on price. They are designed, as are all of the other questions given in this book, to compel the customer to think.

Your goal is to elicit a response from the customer that will promote a meaningful conversation so that a successful conclusion can occur.

**What Questions Do You Ask?**

**Objection: "Your price is way too high."**

**Responses:**

- "Oh?" (This is my favorite.)
- "Really?"
- "I see."
- "Way too high?"
- "Compared to what?"
- "Tell me more."
- "I can appreciate why you may feel that way. How far off would you say I am?"
- "Thank you for sharing this. May I ask what you thought the investment would be?"
- "I'm curious. Why do you feel this way?"
- "You're right. We are the competition in the marketplace, and our pricing reflects our quality. Out of everything you will be receiving with this recommendation, what are you willing to give up in order to have a lower price?"

**Objection: "You need to give me a discount."**

**Responses:**

- "Oh?"
- "A discount?"
- "Why is that?"
- "I do?"
- "I can understand your position. It's important to keep an eye on all expenditures. Since I have given you every discount that I can apply to this program, is this a deal breaker?"
- "What is your decision if I can't give you a discount?"

You have shared your recommendations with the customer as well as answered and overcome all of the customer's objections. The customer has become invested by voicing their suggestions, which will make their final choice for a recommendation a better fit. Now we move to Chapter 11, *Step 7: Gain Agreement and Finalize*.

**Summary:**

**What are the five reasons customers "say" they won't buy from you?**

1. No Need.
2. No Money.
3. No Hurry.
4. No Trust (or Confidence).
5. No Desire.

**Why do customers buy from you instead of your competitor?**

Customers will buy from you over your competitor based on EMOTION.

1. How much the customer likes you over your competitor.
2. How much the customer trusts you over your competitor.
3. How much better you make the customer feel about their buying decision over what your competitor makes the customer feel.

**What is a customer Objection?**

Think of an Objection as active resistance that is voiced by the customer. They want you to prove them wrong and show them how to move forward with your solution successfully.

**What is a Smokescreen?**

Smokescreens happen when the customer doesn't want to admit their real Objection or concern, whether it is their desire to be polite to you, conceal something from your or their own embarrassment.

Chapter Ten

**What is a customer Brush-Off?**

Think of a Brush-Off as a smokescreen that is hiding the real issue.

**How do you defer a customer Objection until you are ready to answer it?**

**ADAPT**
A – Acknowledge
D – Defer
A – And
P – Push
T – Through

**How can you, the salesperson, avoid being responsible for creating customer Objections?**

1. Ask the right questions to uncover customer needs and wants.
2. Ask questions to uncover needs and wants in the right way.
3. Prove the value of your products and services.
4. Connect with the customer, and establish their trust in you as a salesperson.
5. Give the pricing of your recommendation before you give your recommendation.

**What is the strategy to overcome customer Objections and Brush-Offs?**

1. Listen, Listen, Listen.
2. Use Silence.
3. Ask Questions to Draw the Customer Deeper Into their Objection or Brush-Off.

## Chapter 11

## Step 7: Gain Agreement and Finalize

*How to Ask the Customer to Buy and Finalize the Sales Conversation*

Gain Agreement.

When I was twelve, it dawned on me how much I wanted to learn how to whistle like my Dad. My Dad would take his right hand and form a circle with his first finger and his thumb. He would place these two fingers, which formed the circle shape, under his tongue, close his mouth around his fingers, and blow. An extremely loud whistle would be the result. I loved it! I loved my Dad. He was my hero.

However, Dad fell off his hero pedestal once, and it took me a minute to put him back on it. It was when – 20 minutes after getting home from our local bicycle shop with my brand new cobalt blue, Schwinn three-speed bike – I discovered he had spray painted the diagonal bar of my bike with copper spray paint. He

## Chapter Eleven

thought that would make it easier for me to find my bike in the school yard and locate it if it was ever stolen.

Here it comes. My favorite line – what was he thinking? I know exactly what he was thinking. Although a little skewed, Dad was thinking about what was best for me and my brand-new-now-tainted-and-ugly-bike. His heart was in the right place, but his head was simply detached from what was a twelve-year-old girl's reality. True story but I digress. Back to the whistle lesson.

My Dad taught me what to do. I would follow his instructions, and yet, I could not do it for the life of me. Then, one day, Dad said, "You can do this. Let's try it a different way." He taught me to place my two middle fingers together, in an upside down "v," press them on the underside of my tongue, and then blow. I practiced this for about a week. Then, one day I was absentmindedly performing this maneuver and it happened. I created a hollow, sorrowful, howl. But, I did it. Shortly after that, I found the sweet spot and now it's organic. I let it happen and now when I whistle it's loud. I know. I know.

What do these stories have to do with this chapter? Both are completely relevant. The bicycle story is a vivid memory that demonstrates a lack of empathy and just plain insanity. Can you imagine how you would feel if your Dad spray painted your new bike? What about not understanding how his actions caused you to scream and thrash around in the garage like a psycho banshee? Even my mother was dumbfounded and took my side. Now, THAT'S really saying something. In this case Dad's over-protective nature for his daughter caused him to lose sight of the bigger picture.

What about you? Have you ever become so focused on what you thought was best for your customer only to later realize you had strayed far off the path, because you failed to check-in with your customer to see if they were in agreement? This happens, in the beginning, when you are learning the *Don't Sell. Let Them Buy, Sales Conversation Process;* but, one of these events should be enough to shock you into never doing it again. Listen and learn from your customers! They will teach you how to communicate with them.

Okay. Back to the present and how the whistle story relates to this chapter. When I learned the steps of how to whistle and adjusted them to fit what worked for me, I found success. I found that "organic" place, where magic naturally happens. Because it is organic, today, I can still whistle as loudly as ever. Aiden (our Golden Retriever) is as deaf as a post, but he can hear my whistle.

The same is true with the *Don't Sell. Let Them Buy, Sales Conversation Process.* Once you commit the process to organic memory, you naturally move from one step to the next with ease, skill, and focus. You guide instead of pushing your customer to the successful outcome that is right for them.

When you and your customer are at the end of your discussion about how to best implement your products into the customer's business, and you've come to a workable solution over pricing, the next step is to let the customer buy. It should be natural and easy.

The way to do this is from a place of service that comes from a true desire to please your customer, improve their business, and give them a better way of life. You do this through the best products and services you have to offer and with off-the-chart customer service.

The customer may have slight trepidation about actually making that final decision. That's normal, but all of the heavy lifting is over. If you have followed the sales conversation process correctly your customer is by your side wanting your product. because, you have proven to the customer that it IS the right choice for them. And, YOU believe it is the right choice for this customer.

This is the fun part! The hard part is now behind you. You are almost there, and your customer is right there with you. What you now need to do is provide that final assurance to the customer that they are making the right decision. It's not about if they are going to buy, it's about hearing from you that they are making the right decision for their business. They trust you and want your opinion. It feels so good to know you have the ability to help a customer in need, one that now trusts you!

Just keep it simple, easy, and relaxed. Look them right in the eyes and say:

**Example #1 -**

> **You:** "Well, I'm excited for you. Can you see how this system, with your suggested changes, will remove the frustrations you now feel and give you the accountability and productivity you really need?"
>
> **Customer:** "I want to believe it will. But, wow, it's expensive."
>
> **You:** "What is more expensive? Continuing with the frustration and lack of control that you now have, or going with this plan that will be customized to your way of doing business so you finally end the frustration?"

**Customer:** "You really think this will work for us?"

**You:** "Other than my products and services, which I stand behind 100%, and my skill at knowing what solution to offer to clients who have been in your shoes, my reputation is the most important thing I can give to you. Let's do this, and let's do it together."

**Customer:** "You'll be with me?"

**You:** "The whole way."

**Customer:** "Okay. What's next?"

# Example # 2 -

**You:** "You've made some really great changes to this plan, changes that take it to an even more productive level. What do you think your managers will say when you tell them they will have the ability to do "X, Y, and Z?"

**Customer:** "They will be thrilled. They've been asking for this forever."

**You:** "With this implementation, you will keep your team happy, engaged, productive, and accountable, which is exactly what you told me you needed at the very beginning of our conversation."

**Customer:** "It's just unchartered waters."

**You:** "It is for you - for a minute. However, you have me and my team, who will be at the helm until you and your team get your sea legs. We are all here to support you. How does that make you feel?"

**Customer:** "Good, as long as that's the case."

**You:** "That's the case. So, do I have your permission to move forward?"

The point I'm trying to make is be a real person. Talk to your customer as you would want someone to talk to you. Be direct and completely honest. If you have done the right thing for the right reason, all that is left, before you move onto the finalization, is to metaphorically hold the customer's hand. It's time to reassure the customer that their decision is the right decision, and help the customer feel good about that decision. It's that simple.

**Example #3 –**

I want to address the price negotiation that may occur before or during this point in the sales conversation. When you have given every discount that you can think of, and any more cutting of their recommendation would devalue the program, stop and stand your ground. Many times, the price is the price, and it's that price because of the value that your, "whatever" delivers. Enough is enough.

For example. Let's say you are an architect. You have a client that gives you specifications that translate into a home with a price tag of $850,000. Your client about dies and says, "You've got to knock the price down to around $450,000." The only thing you can say is, "Then, I have to give you a choice. Which would you prefer, a box with four rooms and no garage, or deck or, a garage driveway and deck but no house?"

Do not devalue your product for the sake of a sale. Negotiate, yes, but always maintain the integrity of your products, services, and their pricing. Focus on the positives of the features or elements of your program, and not the pricing. What is the customer willing to give up to lower the pricing?

Remember, if price is that big of an issue at this point in the sales conversation, then somewhere along the line you did not prove the value of your product, or you did not qualify the customer as being the right fit for your product.

In the case below, be clear, be direct, and stand your ground.

> **You:** "I'm thrilled for you. Can you see how this system, with your suggested changes, will remove the frustrations you now feel as well as give you the accountability and productivity you really need?"
>
> **Customer:** "I want to believe it will. But, wow, it's expensive. What can you do to lower the price?"
>
> **You:** "Lisa, I know this is a big step for you. We've worked together for over two months and finally created a customized demo that mirrors exactly what you want. You know that I have given you a discount everywhere I can. You know the value of this product because of the testimonials of others who were in your shoes but who have adopted this very system. And, they can't believe it took them so long to implement it. This is what we're down to. Yes, I can cut the rate. But, tell me, who on your team would you like to tell that they will have to wait before there is funding for them to become users on the new CRM system?"
>
> **Customer:** "Nobody! I can't do that."

**You:** "No, of course, you can't. Your entire team needs to move together and share in the excitement of making their work more productive as well as them more accountable, which means higher profits for you.

When this system is implemented, your team will be able to work more efficiently, their frustration level will go down, and you will have happier employees. When people are happy, they are more productive, which means everyone will be making more money. When this happens, you will be asking me to install the other features we discussed to take you to an even higher level of productivity. You are doing the right thing."

**Customer:** "You're sure."

**You:** "I'm 100% sure. My team and I will be right by your side making it all happen. (Say nothing more. Just smile and know how much you are going to help them drastically improve their business.)"

**Finalizing the sales conversation means you will:**

- Complete all necessary contracts and include all pricing and billing guidelines.
- Review the contracts with the customer to ensure their understanding and gain their agreement.
- Explain everything that will happen once you leave, including:
  - Materials the customer will receive.
  - What additional conversations that will take place and with whom.

- Answer additional questions the customer may have.
- Have the customer authorize the contract.
- Sincerely compliment the customer for their decision, and reinforce why their decision is the right decision.
- Express your gratitude for their business and for giving you the opportunity to make a positive difference in their business.

Make it your goal, when working with every customer, to finalize the sales conversation the day you meet with the customer; that way, you won't have to come back, begin again, and lose the momentum you gained during your first conversation. As I stated in Chapter 3, *How to Prepare "Don't Sell. Let Them Buy, Sales Conversations*, you know this as a one-call close. I never liked the term "one-call close." It sounds cold, manipulative, and one-sided in favor of the salesperson.

"Finalizing" the sales conversation aligns the customer with the salesperson. It may seem trivial, but it's a clear mindset that keeps the customer as the focal point. When you "finalize," everything is on the table, reviewed, understood, and agreed upon. A feeling of achievement will come over both you and the customer.

However, you may represent a product where this goal can't be achieved. You may need critical information from your customer to assure yourself that your product is a perfect fit. You may need to take the time to build additional trust with your customer. It may take more meetings and more research, and you may need to demo your product a few more times to others who mysteriously come out of the woodwork. Like the wife, husband or silent partner.

Whatever the case, it is always best to be prepared to finalize the sales conversation at every meeting you have with a customer. This keeps you ready at all times, so when the customer gives you the green light, you seamlessly move to the next steps, whatever those steps may be. And, remember to place white-hot focus on the necessary follow-through to make this a completely positive experience for both your customer and you.

**Steps to Finalizing the Sales Conversation:**

> **Customer:** "This last customized demo you created for us has me convinced. How do we get started?"
>
> **You:** "I am so excited for you and your team. I need to adjust the contract to reflect the changes you want to include. That will take about 15 minutes. Then, you and I will review the contract to make sure we both understand the end goal and are in agreement. I'll also explain what happens next. Where can I go so that I won't be in your way?"
>
> **Customer:** "I have a phone call to make, so why don't you use the conference room down the hall."

You then complete all necessary work. Make any phone calls, if needed, and return to the customer prepared to do a detailed review. This is when salespeople, who have never learned this sales conversation process, get themselves into trouble. Instead of doing a detailed review, they fly over the contract like a plane on the LaGuardia Airport runway; because, they are afraid the customer will have second thoughts when they see the billing and decide to put on the brakes.

Remember, this is now the second time the customer will have seen this billing, or a figure close to this billing because you asked them to write it down before you gave your first recommendation.

The third time they will see the billing is on the contract you give them before you leave their office or when you email the contract to them. The fourth time will be when they receive their first bill. See how this works? You are creating familiarity right from the start. You are already getting the customer used to seeing their billing, so it's not this huge scary thing that comes out of nowhere once you leave their office.

Back to the detailed review.

**Contract Review:**

- Start at the top so the customer can see that you have accurately entered their business contact information.
- Move to each section that has to do with what they purchased. Refresh their memory with:
    - The total billing. (Get that out of the way. It doesn't matter what the price is for the individual items. The last thing you want the customer to do is get caught up in the weeds with individual pricing.)
    - Always recommend in packages or bundles. Keep the customer focused on the program as a whole.
    - What they are purchasing. (Feature)
    - Why they are purchasing it. (Benefit)
- Discuss the terms and conditions, but make it as simple to understand as possible.
    - Be clear.
    - Be honest.

- - o Hide nothing. The reality is still there whether you draw attention to it or not.
- Explain all next steps.
  - o This should be in a form (written or PDF) that they will be able to refer to when and if confusion arises. Never put yourself in the position of the customer saying to you, "You never told me that." Think ahead and prepare. We all have a tendency to remember something the way we want to remember it.
- Ask the customer what questions they may have.
  - o Answer the customer's questions to the best of your ability.
  - o Take notes so you can remember to provide answers promptly once you have left this meeting.
- Have the customer authorize the agreement or contract, and either leave it with them or email it to them.
- Compliment the customer on their decision, and reinforce why their decision will work for them.
- Express your gratitude for:
  - o Their business.
  - o Giving you the opportunity to make a positive difference in their business.

**By following the steps of the Contract Review, you will:**

- Greatly reduce the chance of buyer's remorse.
- Be seen as a complete professional.
- Build more trust with your customer.
- Become more confident in the value of your products and services.

- Become more comfortable when quoting the pricing of your products and propose larger, more successful programs.
- Become more fluid in following every feature with a benefit.
- Make the step of Contract Review organic.

Is this fun, or what?! There is nothing like sharing a great recommendation with a customer when you and they both know your solution is the answer to their need. What will follow is the customer becoming totally invested, invested to the point that they make that recommendation their own. Then, top it all off with a signed contract, an elated customer, and you hitting your sales goal. Both you and your customer will end your sales conversation with a feeling of accomplishment.

You have every right to take a moment to bask in this wonderful feeling…Okay, that's enough. Now you need to follow through on what you promised, and "wow" the socks off your customer with your amazing customer service.

Let's move onto Chapter 12, *Step: 8 Follow-Through – How to Turn a Customer into a Testimonial-Giving, Loyal Fan.*

## Summary:

## Gain agreement by:
- Providing the customer with assurance that they are making the right decision.
- Keeping your conversation direct but also easy and relaxed.
- Complimenting the customer for the suggestions they made to improve your recommendation so it would better fit their needs.
- Asking the customer to envision what positive experience they will feel when this recommendation has been implemented into their business.
- Asking one last direct question that confirms their commitment.

## Steps to Finalizing the Sales Conversation:
## Contract Review:
- Review all:
  - Business contact information.
  - Total billing not individualized items.
  - What they are purchasing. (Feature)
  - Why they are purchasing it. (Benefit)
- Discuss the terms and conditions of the contract.
  - Be clear.
  - Be honest.
  - Hide nothing.
- Explain all next steps.
- Ask the customer what questions they may have.
  - Answer the customer's questions to the best of your ability.
  - Take notes for accurate follow-through.
- Have the customer authorize the agreement.

- Compliment the customer on their decision.
- Reinforce why their decision will work for them.
- Express your gratitude for:
  - Their business.
  - Giving you the opportunity to make a positive difference in their business.

**By following the steps of the Contract Review, you will:**
- Greatly reduce the chance of buyer's remorse.
- Be seen as a complete professional.
- Build more trust with your customer.
- Become more confident in the value of your products and services.
- Become more comfortable when quoting the pricing of your products and propose larger, more successful programs.
- Become more fluid in following every feature with a benefit.
- Make the step of Contract Review organic.

**How to learn how to whistle really loudly**
- Place your two middle fingers together in an upside down "v."
- Press your fingers on the underside of my tongue.
- Blow.
- Keep practicing.
- You will know you are making progress when you begin to make howling sounds.

## Chapter 12

## Step: 8 Follow-Through

### *How to Keep Promises You Make to Your Customers*

It's Monday. The Monday after a glorious Friday with a customer who finally finalized their contract; you've been working with them for the past four months. The glow begins to fade as you realize that you have a videoconference meeting at **8 AM** with your manager and team. You have mounds of CRM data entry to take care of from last pay period's sales and two customer appointments. It's also the beginning of another pay period, which means starting fresh with a new goal to hit. But, there on the end of your desk sits your follow-up notes for the customer's account, whose contract you finalized on Friday.

You have no idea what you promised you would do, and you are praying that you took thorough notes. You are completely overwhelmed with the amount of work in front of you and a new pay period looming over you. What do you do first?

The key to keeping the promises you make to your customers, co-workers, management, and even your family and friends is only to make promises you know you can keep. You have to organize yourself, keep track of those promises, and follow through on what you promise.

**Breathe and take a moment to count your blessings.**

When I'm overwhelmed, I find it very calming to stop and give gratitude for what I have, where it came from, and how it has elevated me. Being grateful and showing gratitude is always the right thing to do.

**Schedule your tasks and daily activities.**

The night before every next sales day, in your CRM, calendar on your phone, or in your Day-Timer, create a schedule for the following day and include every activity that needs to be accomplished. When you begin your day, you won't spin your wheels trying to get organized because you are already organized. Once you've completed a task, check it off, highlight it, do something so you clearly see that the task is completed. This gives you a feeling of accomplishment, because that's exactly what it is; that accomplishment, no matter how small, feels good.

**Time block your week.**

- Carve out specific mornings, afternoons, or whatever amount of time is necessary to take care of:
    o Account preparation and research.
    o Account processing (CRM) and follow-up with other departments.
    o Expressing gratitude to your customers and others who deserve it.
    o Scheduling appointments.

- Scheduling Sales Conversation appointments.
- Attending company meetings.
- Time blocking will:
  - Help you concentrate.
  - Keep you organized.
  - Give you more freedom during your sales day.
  - Help you become more productive.
  - Make you more accountable.
  - Keep your attitude positive.
  - Remove the overwhelm factor.

**Create Detailed Notes for Each Customer's Account.**

Let's take the customer's account you finalized last Friday.

- If your company has not provided you with a CRM or some kind of company follow-through or workflow checklist, you need to create one. It will:
  - Keep you on schedule.
  - Remind you of what promises you made to your customers, and help monitor your progress in fulfilling those promises.
  - Help you to know when to engage or follow up with the people in your processing department who need to touch the customer's account as well.
  - Ensure you won't miss a crucial step in the processing of their account.
  - Keep you organized.
  - Help you think of more efficient ways to process a customer's account.
  - Remind you when you need to reach out to the customer to give a progress report.

## Chapter Twelve

Treat the processing of every account as if it were your account. Pay attention to detail. Hold yourself, and others, accountable for 100% accuracy. Let nothing fall through the cracks. Set a timetable for completion, and stick to it. If something breaks down in the processing of the account, find out where the breakdown happened and monitor the correction. It doesn't do any good to place blame. Just focus on the solution, and fix it. Your support team will realize how serious you are about accountability and accuracy.

Show your support team respect for what they do. Express your gratitude. They will be more likely to pay closer attention when they process your accounts. Stay in front of any potential issues. Meet them head-on, and solve the problem. It will still be there when you are forced to finally handle it, so just get it solved before things get out of hand and you run out of time.

Stay in front of your customer, and update them on a consistent basis; avoid letting time pass until the point the customer has to call you to learn about progress on their account. Communication that you initiate will continue to create trust and a valued relationship beyond your sales conversation meeting.

It's really very simple. If you promise your customer you will do something, do it. Then go a step or two further to surprise them with a "special" something that makes their day. This is what will help make you the competition and set you apart from your competitors. Continue to give them value through your actions. You will have created a loyal fan that will continue to trust you, be willing to buy more from you in the future, and be proud to refer you to their colleagues.

**Summary:**

**Breathe and take a moment to count your blessings.**
**How to keep your promises to your customers:**
- Take great notes while in your sales conversations.
- Organize the notes and create action items with scheduled times for completion.
- Log notes into your CRM system, phone calendar, or Day Timer. This will:
  o Keep you on schedule.
  o Remind you of what promises you made to your customers and help monitor your progress in fulfilling those promises.
  o Help you to know when to engage or follow up with the people in your processing department who need to touch the customer's account as well.
  o Ensure you won't miss a crucial step in the processing of their account.
  o Keep you organized.
  o Help you think of more efficient ways to process a customer's account.
  o Remind you when you need to reach out to the customer to give a progress report.
- Treat the processing of every account as you would want a salesperson to do for you if you were the customer.
- Pay attention to detail.
- Hold yourself, and others, accountable for 100% accuracy.
- Let nothing fall through the cracks.
- Set a timetable for completion and stick to it.

- If something breaks down in the processing of the account, find out where the breakdown happened and monitor the correction.
- Focus on fixing the breakdown and avoid placing blame.
- Stay in front of any potential issues. Meet them head-on and solve the problems.

**Time block your week:**

- Carve out specific mornings, afternoons, or whatever amount of time is necessary to take care of:
    - Account preparation and research.
    - Account processing (CRM) and follow-up with other departments.
    - Expressing gratitude to your customers and others who deserve it.
    - Scheduling appointments.
    - Scheduling Sales Conversation appointments.
    - Attending company meetings.

**Time blocking will:**
- Help you concentrate.
- Keep you organized.
- Give you more freedom during your sales day.
- Help you become more productive.
- Make you more accountable.
- Keep your attitude positive.
- Remove the overwhelm factor.

Promise only what you can deliver. Deliver. Then, surprise your customer with something more. Be a force to be reckoned with. BE the competition.

## Chapter 13

## Step 9: Show Gratitude

### *How to Create Loyal Fans*

Why should you be grateful? For anything? Foolish question, right? It is when you only look at one side.

**Side one – Show Gratitude
Because It's the Right Thing to Do.**

My Mother was not only a registered nurse but the director of nursing and assisting staff at what was, at that time, the largest facility in the country for the mentally disabled.

When I was eight years old, there was a woman, Mrs. Martin, who worked on Mom's staff and adored my Mother. One of the ways she showed her gratitude to my Mom (and, let's be honest, maybe to butter her up a little) was to bring things for her to give to me – a baggy of gum balls, other goodies, or little plastic toys.

## Chapter Thirteen

I didn't know this at the time, but her husband was in the vending machine business and filled the gum ball machines you see at the front doors of supermarkets. To receive this bag of fun treasures was an absolute thrill for me.

One day, Mom came home with the bag, and I (of course) jumped and squealed all over the kitchen. But, my Mom sat me down; she told me that Mrs. Martin's husband had passed away and that this was probably the last bag I would receive. She explained that he was the one who made those bags for me. And, now, he was in heaven and free from the pain he was feeling. She told me that Mrs. Martin was sad and would miss him, but she would find her way.

It was then that it hit me. I never stopped to thank Mrs. Martin and now Mr. Martin (who was gone) for all of the wonderful treasures they had given me. I could, however, write a note to Mrs. Martin. Mom later told me that my note had brightened her day and that she was touched that I thought to write it.

Years later, when I had my driver's license and was allowed to drive me and my best friend (Paula) to high school, I was responsible for picking up Mom at the end of her day. One afternoon, I walked into Mom's office, and there was Mrs. Martin.

I swear, she looked like she was 102 years old, even though she was probably in her late 50's or early 60's. (Age has such a different perspective when you're in your teens. But, then again, when you're in your late 50's, people at the age of 60 don't look that old. How does that happen?)

She stood up, hugged me and said, "Miss Chiqeeta, I will always remember the note you sent to me. I was in such an awful place. You gave me hope through your kindness and gratitude. Mr. Martin would have been so pleased to know you appreciated his thoughtfulness." Since I wear my feelings on my sleeve, I broke down and cried all over Mrs. Martin while I hugged her.

My small expression of gratitude, an action that both Mom and Dad had tried to instill in me, really meant something to Mrs. Martin. That moment has stayed with me. I've tried to remember why it's important to give thanks to God, to the Universe, or to the higher power you believe exists. And, openly express gratitude to others so I can uplift them and give them the appreciation they deserve or may need to hear. Taking the time to express your gratitude is the perfect example of doing the right thing for the right reason – it's just the right thing to do.

Post Script – My Grandma Gertie always said, "Crying is good for you. It airs the soul and the more you cry, the less you pee." Yep, I'm from the Midwest, alright?

**Side Two – Show Gratitude and Create Loyal Fans.**

You have taken a lot of time to build relationships with your customers. Then, reality sets in, and time gets away from you. There are new customers to see and other relationships to forge. What? Already? It's time to renew the contracts of your previous customers? You realize that months have gone by without making contact. How many customers is that? Oh well, this will be a slam-dunk. Think again.

What if, while you were moving on, your competition snuck in and stole your customers away from you? It could happen, and it does happen.

What have you done to show your gratitude and provide the service your customers deserve, the kind of service that keeps them loyal to you and not migrating to your competition?

Let me share some basic and creative ways to help you develop loyal customers and fans.

**Handwritten Note:**

A handwritten thank you note never goes out of style, especially when most salespeople don't even think of doing it anymore. It's easier and faster to send a thank you in an email. (Do you even bother to send a thank you email?) Yes, it is. But, this is the norm now and not the exception. And, to be honest, it feels like a shortcut.

Be different, stand out, and make someone's day. Receiving something in the mail that is not considered junk mail, bills, catalogs or solicitations for charities – even though most companies are going paperless – is a rarity. I love getting handwritten thank you notes from my nieces and sister-in-law. I know this act of gratitude was passed on by Nancy (my mother-in-law) to Marni (my sister-in-law), who then passed it onto her girls (Paige and Marissa).

I'm thrilled to have proof that people still write! It's a lovely gesture; it warms my heart to get an expression of gratitude from my precious girls. I hope it's a gesture that never goes away. The only thing that comes close is when I receive a thank you from my clients and, of course, my amazing husband. It validates that what I'm doing makes a difference. We all need that every once in a while.

**When to send a handwritten business "thank you" note:**

1. After your initial sales conversation. This makes sense when:
   - You know you are in competition with other competitors.
   - There is lag-time before your customer can give you an answer.
   - You were only able to meet with one of the decision-makers. This will help you win an ally over to your side when you meet with the other decision-makers.
2. After the customer has signed their contract with you.
3. You went back to the customer to share an up-sell or cross-sell opportunity, and the customer bought what you had to offer.
4. After the customer gave you a testimonial.
5. After the customer gave you a referral to a colleague.

**When to send a handwritten note…"just because."**

1. Remember conversations with your customers and acknowledge:
   - Birthdays.
   - Special Occasions.
   - Events that your customers participate in and are passionate about.
2. Send a note when you send a promised item.
3. Send a note when you send something that could be of interest to your customer, and you are doing so just because it's a nice thing to do.

In this day and age, expressing your gratitude is, sadly, a welcomed surprise instead of the norm. So, make someone's day.

## What to say in your handwritten note:

Inspiration for this section comes from Tom Hopkins, one of the world's most influential sales trainers, speakers, and authors. Mr. Hopkins is also known for being one of the nicest, most gracious people you will ever meet.

Mr. Hopkins published an article online entitled, *Sending Thank You Notes.*[1] I urge you to read it to get additional ideas on how to craft thank you notes that fit your personality.

Here are a few of my suggestions on what to say in a thank you note, for various situations. You are welcome to use them or modify these suggestions in a way that better fits your writing style.

### After the Initial Sales Conversation –

*Thank you for scheduling the time to meet with me (insert yesterday, the day of the week, or whatever). It was a pleasure to have an in-depth conversation and learn more about you and your company.*

*I look forward to being given the opportunity to further discuss how my products can be of service to you. As you requested, I will follow up with a phone call at the end of next week. Thank you again for your time.*

### After a Purchase –

*I want to congratulate you on your investment in (insert whatever the customer purchased from you)! You are now a part of the (your company's name) team. Our goal is to provide you with the best possible service, so you are continually assured that you have made the right business decision, at this point in time, for what is to come in the future.*

## Asking for a Referral –

*It is always nice talking with you. It is especially great to hear that you are so pleased with my (insert whatever product or service you represent) and service. Since you are experiencing success, may I ask you for a referral – to a colleague of yours who may have similar needs and also be interested in learning about my products and services?*

*You have my word that I will provide them with the highest standard of customer service, the same level of service that I aim to provide to you.*

## After Meeting with a Referral –

*Thank you for your referral of Steve Customer.*

*Your generosity has given me the opportunity to serve someone else in need of my (insert whatever you represent); you have helped Steve get on the path to solving some of the same issues with which you have struggled. I want you to know that I appreciate your business and your referral to Mr. Customer.*

## After the Customer Decided not to Buy But May Do So in the Future –

*Thank you for taking the time to learn about my (insert whatever you represent). I am saddened to know that I have not been given the opportunity to serve and work with you.*

*However, I will keep you apprised of further developments in my products and services, which may be of benefit to you, and look forward to the possibility of serving you in the future. Know that I am here for you. Please call me, anytime.*

## Chapter Thirteen

**After the Customer Bought from a Competitor –**

*Thank you for taking the time to learn about my (insert whatever you represent). I sincerely regret that I was unable to prove the value my product has to offer. I wish you the very best success and look forward to the possibility of doing business together in the future.*

**Send Short Videos From Your Phone.**

This idea comes from Mike Koenigs, eleven-time #1 Bestselling Author, serial entrepreneur, filmmaker, international speaker, and patented inventor. Mike is always thinking outside of the box. In his book, *Money Phone*[2], he talks about how to advance your sales career using your cell phone. My favorite is the simplicity of saying, "thank you," using a text video. It's a great idea and is wonderfully unexpected by your clients.

(You can get a copy of *Money Phone* for free when you go to **www.GoMoneyPhone.com**.)

1. **Send a selfie video to:**
   - Say thank you.
   - Acknowledge special occasions and events.
   - Share when you encounter something that would be of interest to your customer.

**What Your Company Can Do to Show Gratitude and Create Customer Loyalty**

I ran across a really useful article on the Internet, written by Allison Canty, Customer Engagement Manager at Grasshopper (acquired by Citrix).

**Ms. Canty states:**

> *...I'm always looking for ways to make our customers happy. So happy in fact, that when a competitor comes calling with a better deal, they're not even tempted....*
>
> *...I've heard a lot of people say that it's too expensive to go the extra mile to turn customers into fans or that they're just one person and don't have enough time. (CHOO...CHOO, HERE COMES THE EXCUSE EXPRESS!) It doesn't take a ton of time nor does it have to cost you an arm and a leg to show customers you care.*
>
> *It's the same as being a good friend—sitting on your sofa having a heart-to-heart can be more powerful than an expensive girls' night out.* **Simply put: a little love can go a long way."**[3]

You go, girl! I completely agree!

Here are some examples that Ms. Canty suggests for your company to create and maintain loyal customer fans. She and her colleagues at Grasshopper are feeling the success after implementing these ideas. You and your company, will too!

1. **Feature Your Customers on Your Website.**
   - Create a customer page to highlight your customers and what they do.
   - Share your customers' great reviews.
2. **Feature Your Customers in your company blog and social media outlets.**
3. **Invite your customers to post on your blog. (This will take monitoring, but the benefits can be worth it.)**
4. **Include your customers in events, conferences, or whatever you are doing for outreach.**

5. **Send thank you videos when your customers complete a form on your website or give your company a great review.**

There are many more ways to show gratitude. The point is to take the time to do so.

**Summary:**

**The Two Sides of Why to Express Gratitude:**
- It's the right thing to do.
- You create loyal customer fans.

**When to Send a Handwritten Business "Thank You" Note:**
1. After your initial sales conversation.
2. After the customer has signed their contract with you.
3. After you go back to the customer to share an up-sell or cross-sell opportunity, and the customer bought what you had to offer.
4. After the customer gave you a testimonial.
5. After the customer gave you a referral to a colleague.
6. After you met with the referral who bought from you.

**When to Send a "Just Because" Handwritten Note:**
1. Birthdays.
2. Special Occasions.
3. Events that your customers participate in and are passionate about.
4. When you send a promised item.
5. When you send something that would be of interest to your customer.
6. After the customer decided not to buy from you.

7. After you learned the customer purchased from your competitor.

**Send Short Videos From Your Phone.**
- Send a selfie video to:
  - Say, "thank you."
  - Acknowledge special occasions and events.
  - When you encounter something that would be of interest to your customer.

**Ways Your Company Can Show Gratitude and Create Customer Loyalty:**

1. Feature Your Customers on Your Website.
2. Create a customer page to highlight your customers and what they do.
3. Share your customers' great reviews.
4. Feature Your Customers in your company blog and social media outlets.
5. Invite your customers to post on your blog.
6. Include your customers in events, conferences, or whatever you are doing for outreach.
7. Create "thank you" videos when your customers complete a form on your website or give your company a great review.

---

[1] *Sending Thank You Notes* by **Tom Hopkins** – Published in How to Selling Skills June 18, 2014 http://www.tomhopkins.com/blog/tag/thank-you-notes

[2] *Money Phone,* by **Mike Koenigs** Copyright 2017 Published by Mike Koenigs and You Everywhere Now.com

[3] *7 Ways to Turn Your Customers into Huge Fans* by **Allison Canty** – Published in Getting Started on Nov 5, 2013 **http://www.grasshopper.com/blog/7-ways-to-turn-your-customers-into-huge-fans/**

Chapter Thirteen

## Chapter 14

### *Final Thoughts from the Author*

I come from a small town in Lincoln, Illinois - population 14,000. My Mom, Dorothy, was of a German/Protestant descent and Dad, Steve, was Croatian/Catholic lineage.

Mom was a registered nurse and director of nursing at (the now closed) Lincoln State School for the Mentally Handicapped. It was once the largest facility of its kind. She was also the first woman to be elected church elder in the history of the First Cumberland Presbyterian Church. Mom was 100% devoted to her church. Not once, in my life, did I ever hear her exclaim an obscenity. She didn't have to. You'll understand why shortly.

Mom was the first one at church to make sure the coffee was ready on Sundays and for Wednesday prayer meetings. She was the pianist and the Sunday School teacher who led the Mary Martha Class or as Dad would refer to as the Holy Jesus Mary Martha Club. Mom was loved, respected and a lot of fun.

## Chapter Fourteen

Dad was a commercial contractor. Later in life, he opened a men's suit shop. (It was really a place for him and his buddies to have a place to go.). He was also an alderman on the city council and a regular at the Mel O Crème Donut Shop. On Friday nights after dinner, he would take Mom to shop at Wal-Mart while he drank coffee and gave counsel to the employees, who loved to hear his stories when they were on break.

Dad did not have a college education, but he was street-smart, hot-headed, and always known for helping those in need. He was one of the wisest people I've ever known and always told my sister and me that he graduated from the school of hard knocks.

My sister, Quita, always wanted a sibling. But, I was born when Mom and Dad were both 44 years old and two months after they had sent my sister off to college.

What my parents went through with me. Ugh! So, I grew up with parents who were the age of all my friend's grandparents and with a sister who (I love her to pieces) was saddled with being both sister and mother to me. I owe Sissy (my nickname for Quita) and her husband, George Shier (Bro), for putting up with me all these years. Let me digress to clear something up.

My sister's name is "Quita." Eighteen years later I come along, and I'm named "Chiqeeta." Then, Quita names her daughter "Anita." Thank God, I didn't have kids because I was not going down that path. Quita is named after a friend of Mom and Dad's. And, guess whom I'm named after…. a Puerto Rican gang member who worked for my dad when Dad was a master welder and the foreman of the San Pedro Ship Yard during World War II. Dad said she was rougher than a cob and a hard worker. He loved her name, so I'm of Croatian descent with a Puerto Rican name that is misspelled, on purpose. Thank you, Dad.

There is no "u" in my name because he thought people would mispronounce it. Right. YOU go through life being constantly reminded that your name is misspelled. And, let's not forget, "Hey, did you know you share the same name as a banana? Chiquita bananas and I come to say…" Millennials, you have no idea what I'm referring to – Do you?

And, there's one more thing about my name. Around fourth grade, I'd about had it with the teasing about my weird name. One night at the dinner table, I asked Mom and Dad why they gave me such a stupid name. Mom looked at Dad with that you-take-this-one glance. Dad was quietly eating his dinner.

He didn't look up, but he said, "How many little girls do you know that are named 'Debbie?'"

I thought for a moment and said, "Three."

Dad then said, "How about Sue or Susie?"

I thought for a second and said, "Two."

Then, Dad (in his infinite wisdom) said, "And, how many girls do you know with the same name as yours?"

I immediately said, "Nobody." Dad just kept eating but was looking directly at me and smiling. That's when it hit me. My name was unique, not stupid.

Dad then said, "You were a gift from God to your mother and me. That's why we wanted to give you a name that was special, one that no other little girl would have. Be grateful for your beautiful name and live up to it. Mom and I love you. Do you believe that?"

Of course, I started to cry. I understood and, from that day on, I have loved my name although I still have to explain it. I now do it with that loving memory in mind.

## Chapter Fourteen

I miss my folks so much sometimes that I can't breathe. I hear Dad in something I've just said, or I hear Mom tell me that I've added too much water in my pie crust as I'm making an apple pie. Then, the memories come flooding back.

I remember Mom calling Dad and me (when I was in grade school) to dinner at about 5:45 PM. (You're still on the freeway with 45 minutes more before you even see your neighborhood, right?) The front door would be standing wide open. (Not today! Our door here in LA has two deadbolts. There was a front screen door though.) A gentle breeze would be blowing through the house with the back door open creating a cross breeze. (Are you kidding?) The amazing aroma of potatoes and onions frying in bacon grease. (No way, Ahhhh!) It was absolute heaven. (Now it's known as a heart attack!)

Mom, Dad and I would sit in our designated seats, at the little round kitchen table, and I would say grace. At the end, Dad would say, "Me too."

After a few minutes of savoring Mom's incredible cooking – except when she steamed broccoli, when you're a kid, broccoli is just plain evil – Dad would say to me, in his Croatian accent, "So, what mark did you leave on the world today, Hot Rock?"

Hot Rock was Dad's nickname for me. I have very long legs. He always said that, when he would watch me dance, I looked like a Crane on a hot rock. Now, that brings to mind an attractive sight – doesn't it?

Moving on, what Dad meant was, did I help or hurt, someone or something by what I said or did. When he asked me this question, I would tend to unload whatever the day's events were. I blabbed on and on. I sucked all of the oxygen out of the room. At school, I was insecure and lacked all sense of confidence.

I felt that I was the one everyone would stare at and notice how awkward I was. I never felt like I fit in, and I continually doubted myself. Thank God for my best friend Paula, or Red, as Dad would call her because of her beautiful red hair, whom I met in fifth grade.

She was my shield all through grade school and into high school. Today, I feel so fortunate to still have her shoulder to lean on and for the laughter we enjoy during each conversation because of the history we share.

Mrs. Smock, my eighth-grade teacher, must have seen my lack of self confidence because, on the last day of $8^{th}$ grade, she called me to her desk. (OMG! I was petrified. I thought that she was going to tell me I had to repeat $8^{th}$ grade. Why do we think like that?) She gave me a piece of paper. Written on it was "Dan McLaughlin, Speech Teacher, and Coach." She told me that I needed to meet him when I got to high school in the fall and to learn about the Speech Team.

Mrs. Smock's act of devotion, her commitment to her work and her students, sent me on a path with direction and purpose. Dan accepted me onto the Speech Team. (And, of course, every other student who wanted to be on the team. But, I didn't know that.) He guided me to prose and poetry reading competitions. I loved these events; I loved competing.

Are you kidding? I loved winning! He made me rehearse. But, he gave me a choice. Dan said to me, "How much effort you put into rehearsal will show in your final performance. You either commit to being the best you can be, or you settle for being one of the crowd. Which do you choose?" It was Dan McLaughlin, the best school teacher and coach I have ever had, who gets the credit for pulling me out of my shell.

## Chapter Fourteen

I will forever be grateful for his guidance, patience, and constant kicks in the rear-end. Because of Dan's willingness to put up with my insecurities and his good-now-do-it-agains, when it was time for college, I auditioned for the Illinois State Forensics Team and earned a four-year scholarship.

I had no idea, until much later, how much this financial aid helped my parents. I am truly grateful for being an ISU scholarship recipient. I attribute the ISU Speech Team experience to the foundation of my sales success.

It all began though, at home where I felt free. I felt loved and protected. My parents always told me that they believed in me and that I could become anything I wanted to be.

So, as I write this last chapter, it saddens me to know that I can't share this book with Mom and Dad. If I could, I know exactly what would happen and the scene that would take place at our kitchen table in my childhood home in Lincoln, Illinois.

It's about 4:30 PM on a Saturday. The kitchen fills with the aroma of Mom's famous, fresh out of the oven, 1-2-3 shortbread cookies. (They melt in your mouth.) Front and back doors are open with that summer breeze blowing through the house. Dad is drinking black coffee, loaded with sugar, out of a thin china cup. As he stirs, the clinking of the spoon, as it hits the sides of the china cup, echoes in the little kitchen. Dad looks into his coffee then up and directly at me. (I have Dad's eyes. He always said my eyes look like two-burnt-holes-in-a-blanket. Now that brings to mind a horror film, doesn't it?)

Dad asks, "So, what mark did you leave on the world today, Hot Rock?"

I look at Dad and say, "Dad, I have tried to put my 30 plus years of sales experience into a book and online…"

"What the hell. Why would you put a book on a clothes line?" he would say. I can hear him now.

"Never mind. I wrote a book. Focus, focus on the book."

"You wrote a book! Well, I'll be @! # damned!" Dad says.

"Dad! Don't take the Lord's name in vain!" Mom exclaims.

"Ha! You wrote a @! # dang book? Well, I'll be…" says Dad.

"Yes. Now, just listen, okay?" OMG! Nothing changes. It's just as I remember. It's home, and it feels great, even with the profanity. Dad had such a command of the English language.

I continue, "It's a book for salespeople who have lost their way."

"What da ya mean they lost their way? Give 'em a @! # dang map," Dad says, making a joke.

"Actually, Dad, that's what I did." The phone rings. Mom gets up to answer it.

"Oh, for cryin' out loud. Never fails. Ma, let the damn ring," says Dad.

"I can't do that! What if somebody needs help?" Mom replies.

"They don't know you're here," Dad says.

"I know I'm here!" Mom says, exasperated

"Oh, for God's sake…" Dad says as he bangs his hand on the table. I can hear the familiar clang of the big ring Dad always wore on his right hand as it hit the table. When he was 25 years old, Dad sold appliances for the Central Illinois Public Service Company. That ring was presented to him in 1937 for being the top salesperson in the company.

## Chapter Fourteen

"Dad, will you quit saying that?" Mom exclaims. Then, she looks at me and says, "Don't say any more till I get off the phone. I want to hear this." Mom points a finger at Dad and says, "Hello?"

"Tell em' you'll call em' back. We got excitement here," says Dad.

Mom tells Aunt Nettie, her sister-in-law, that she'll call her back. Dad dunks his cookie in the coffee and says, "So, your book is like a Rand McNally road map?"

"Yeah, Dad." I say. "That's a pretty good analogy. It's a structure or a process for the way a salesperson has a conversation with a customer. If the salesperson follows this process, every time, the same way and without fail, they won't get lost or thrown off when the customer says something out of left field. The process or structure will keep the salesperson organized, on track, and confident."

Mom chimes in to say, "Honey, that sounds wonderful! I'm so proud of you! Why did you decide to write this?"

"All my life, you and Dad have taught me to search for my purpose, leave a mark, and make a positive difference. I have proven, in my own sales career, that this process works. So, I thought why not share what I have learned with other salespeople who are struggling as I did or with those who want to hone their selling skills. So, I wrote a book and I will be launching it online...."

"Why do you keep bringing up a clothesline? Or, are you talking about the telephone line? What the hell are you talking about?" says Dad.

"Sorry, nothing; I meant in written form, whatever," I say not wanting to go there.

"How did you come up with this map structure?" asks Dad.

"It's a compilation of what I have learned over the years from you, Mom, and a lot of really successful salespeople," I say.

"Yeah? Mom and Me?" Dad says taken off guard.

"Yes, you and Mom! You taught me how to be of service to others. You taught me how much more fulfilling life can be when you focus on the needs of others. You taught me to figure out how to help people have a better way of life. But, most importantly, you taught me that doing the right thing for the right reason is never wrong," I say.

Dad looks down, and I can tell that my words of gratitude have touched him. Mom is silently crying and wiping her eyes with one of her many embroidered handkerchiefs.

Dad clears his throat, picks up my book, and asks, "So, this title, *'Don't Sell. Let Them Buy,'* That's catchy. I like that."

A sad smile crosses my face, and I remember exactly where the inspiration for my book title came from. I say, "It breaks my heart that you did not get the chance to meet the dear, wonderful man who gave me this idea. You two would get along like two peas in a pod."

"Neal Jameson, my father-in-law, and I were talking in the family room of the home he shared with Nancy, his wife of over 50 years. At one point, Dad Jameson looked at me and quietly said, 'Honey, what makes you a success at sales is that you don't sell people, you let them buy.''

"Oh, what a nice man he must have been," Mom says.

"He certainly was," I say. Then, "So, Dad, would you like to read my book?"

## Chapter Fourteen

"Why the heck would I do that? I don't need to learn how to sell anything. Besides, you said it's based on what I taught you anyway. I already know what's in there," he says.

I just smile and shake my head knowing that Mom will read every word of my book to Dad after I've gone.

Mom read to Dad all my life. I just accepted it as normal. I would come home or wander into the kitchen, from who knows where, and find Mom and Dad at the kitchen table. Dad would be slurping soggy coffee-soaked Corn Flakes off a spoon as Mom read the newspaper to him. They would discuss and debate what they had both just learned from the Lincoln Courier. That was "home" to me.

One day, about 4:45 PM and two months after Dad had passed, Mom and I were sitting at the kitchen table. Mom was grieving terribly. With tears streaming down her face, she was talking quietly to herself, as if she had forgotten I was there.

I heard her say, "Oh Dad. I miss you so much. I keep waiting for you to walk in the door so I can read the paper to you."

Mom then looked up and said, "Do you know why I always read to your dad?"

As I silently cried, and with as much composure as I could muster, I said, "No, Mom. Why?"

"Your dad was dyslexic. That's why he dropped out of school after the eighth grade. He would become so frustrated and embarrassed. All our married life, I tried to ease his suffering by reading to him. It was our special time. He never wanted you or your sister to know."

Then I said, "I had no idea Dad was dyslexic. How did he work?"

"It was a struggle, but Dad surrounded himself with good people who helped him," Mom said.

"But, how did he get through the test for the GED?" I said.

Mom was quiet. Staring into her favorite coffee mug that Dad bought for her from the local Holiday Inn, she said, "I helped your dad study for his GED, late at night when you were in bed, for a year. He also went to night school to prepare."

"What? I had no idea," I said. My heart ached for Dad while bursting with pride that he attained his quiet goal.

I was in grade school the day Dad took the GED test, I remembered seeing him in his blue polyester suit, white shirt and a red tie so wide you could land an airplane on it. Dad resembled Ronald Regan. He looked handsome and rattled. Mom took his face in her hands and said, "Dad, you can do this. Have faith that you are ready and ask God to be with you."

Dad was at least 30 years older than the other students in his night class. Dad's night class instructor was also the proctor for the exam. She could see that Dad was extremely nervous and struggling to comprehend the words on the page. The instructor walked over to Dad, placed her hand on his shoulder and said, "Steve, breathe. It's okay."

Dad, in a shaky voice, said, "The words. They're jumping all over the place."

The proctor then said, "You can do this Steve. I know you know this material. Just breathe deeply when the words begin to jump."

Tears began to run down Dad's cheeks which angered and embarrassed him.

Then, the proctor said, "Use the anger, Steve. Then, let it go. The answer to the first question is 'B.' The answer to number two is 'A,'" Dad later told Mom how compassionate and supportive the instructor had been. Her advice had helped him settle so he could read the words on the page.

Weeks later, the letter from the Department of Education came in the mail. Mom and I were waiting for Dad to get home for him to open it. When Dad walked in, Mom gave Dad the letter. He pushed the letter back at Mom and said, "Mom, you open it."

Mom opened the envelope, took out the letter and began to read. "Congratulations! You have successfully passed your GED." Her face broke into a huge smile, and she began to cry. Then, she turned the letter around so Dad could see it.

Tears spilled down his cheeks. Then, he said, "Look Ma. I got 'A.' I got 'A."

Back to my fantasy – present time.

Then, Dad says, "How many copies you got with you?"

"A few. Why?" I say.

"I need me about 30 copies, and I want them all signed so I can pass them out. I'll start at Wal-Mart. There are a lot of young people out there who need help, so let's help them."

I say, "Dad, no…"

Mom cuts me off, "Honey, let it go. You know your Dad. You've just given him a new mission. We are both so proud of you," Mom says.

Mom and Dad were married for 52 years. They were wonderful parents who loved my precious sister and me unconditionally. I am so grateful for their love, guidance, and the values that I now embrace in my life.

By sharing a little about my personal history and my upbringing with you, perhaps you can better understand who I am, and where my personal and professional values originated.

It is my hope that something I've said within this book resonates with you. My goal is to help you learn why something is not working in your sales conversation and show you how to correct whatever part of your sales conversation may need attention.

I would love to hear your thoughts and answer questions you may have. Please feel free to reach out to me at
cj@chiqeetajameson.com.

You can also contact me through my website at
www.ChiqeetaJamesom.com.

I'm here to serve. How can I be of service to you?

Chapter Fourteen

Don't Sell. Let Them Buy.™

## Steps of the Don't Sell. Let Them Buy™ Sales Conversation Process

# References:

**Chapter One:**

1. **Adkins, Amy.** (2016). U.S. Employee Engagement Steady in June. *Workplace,* Gallup Daily, June 1-30. Retrieved from http://www.gallup.com/poll/193901/employee-engagement-steady-june.aspx?g_source=Employee+engagement+2016&g_medium=search&g_campaign=tiles

2. **Dyer, Wayne. (n. d.).** Wayne's Blog. [Web log post] Success Secrets. Retrieved from http://www.drwaynedyer.com/blog/success-secrets/

**Chapter Two:**

1. **Ziglar, Zig.** Secrets of Closing the Sale. Grand Rapids, Michigan: Revell.

**Chapter Three:**

# References

1. **Provide Support, LLC**. (2015, February 20). "Shocking Customer Service Facts and Stats (Infographic)." [LinkedIn]. *SlideShare*. Retrieved from https://www.slideshare.net/ProvideSupport/upload-f118o34o7pif5jgq39reokpfc6219937final

**Chapter Four:**

1. **Burg, B., & Mann, J.D**. (2010). *Go-Givers Sell More*. New York, NY: Penguin Group.

**Chapter Nine:**

1. **Appleton, D.** (1932). *The Rhetoric of Aristotle: An Expanded Translation with Supplementary Examples for Students of Composition and Public Speaking.* New York, NY: Prentice Hall.

2. **Shaw, B. (n.d.).** George Bernard Shaw Quotes. *BrainyQuote*. Retrieved from https://www.brainyquote.com/quotes/quotes/g/georgebern121841.html

**Chapter Thirteen:**

1. *Sending Thank You Notes* by **Tom Hopkins** – Published in How to Selling Skills June 18, 2014
http://www.tomhopkins.com/blog/tag/thank-you-notes

2. *Money Phone,* by Mike Koenigs Copyright 2017 Published by **Mike Koenigs** and You Everywhere Now.com

3. *7 Ways to Turn Your Customers into Huge Fans* by **Allison Canty** – Published in Getting Started on Nov 5, 2013
http://www.grasshopper.com/blog/7-ways-to-turn-your-customers-into-huge-fans/

## Acknowledgements & Expressions of Gratitude

This book would not have been possible had it not been for the support and guidance I have received from so many friends, colleagues and business associates over the years. This book would not have been possible if I had not listened to those who knew more than I did and who helped me find my own path to understanding and ultimately success, in learning the importance of "giving to" rather than "taking from," others. I learned that the universal law of attraction is that whatever you give forth, you will ultimately attract.

Steve and Dorothy Verban, my parents, for providing me with a loving family upbringing, a strong Midwest foundation of values and hilarious memories that will always make me smile. I miss you every day.

Dr. Kevin Kelly, the doctor who saved my life because he was the only physician out of six, who educated me about dense-breast tissue, questioned my mammograms, and used ultrasound to discover the cancer that had been in my breast for over a year. I'm able to take this journey because of you. I believe in you, Dr. Kelly and your amazing SonoCiné AWBUS technology. Thank you for prolonging my life. **www.SonoCine.com**

Neal and Nancy Jameson, for bringing into the world, your son, Craig Allen, for accepting me into your family and for your insight, Dad, during an afternoon conversation, "Honey, you don't sell people, you let them buy." Thank you, Dad. I miss our weekend visits with you and Mom.

Craig Jameson, my amazingly talented and brilliant husband for your patience in accepting me as I am (with all of my idiosyncrasies and craziness) and for your belief and unconditional support in what I'm trying to do.

## Acknowledgements & Gratitude

Quita and George Shier, my sister and brother-in-law, for your love, support (in so many ways) and for the balance you bring to my life.

Andrew, Niki, Arianna and Talia Shier, my nephew and family for your love and constant support.

Janet Wood and Dr. Jay Silverman, our dear friends, for your consistent flow of positive energy, enthusiasm, love and 100% support. We love you!

Stacey Williams, my dear friend, Perennial sister and the master of all power point creators, for your never-ending willingness to help me every time I ask.

Lisa Bollow, my incredible marketing and business strategist. I could not do what I'm doing without your guidance and expertise. I know you truly care because of how well you are overseeing every aspect of my business and the publishing of this book. You are a God-send.

Alexis Kerr, my incredibly talented editor who lets my voice sing through the words on the page but whom, thank God, corrects my grammar and punctuation so I don't look like and idiot.

Joana Kimsey, right arm and assistant to Lisa Bollow for keeping the path clear for our Lisa.

Rebekah Riggs, the other right arm of Lisa Bollow for your dedication to my cause and keeping all marketing materials in order and rolling along.

My Pinnacle Mastermind group, Lola Kakes, Cathy Fitzpatrick, Andrea Jensen and Paulette Dillon for holding me accountable, pushing me to be the best I can be and giving me a shoulder to lean on when all heck breaks loose.

Giles Fabris, my Mastermind Coach, who is always available to listen, mentor and provide a stiff kick in the rear-end when needed.

Bob Burg and John David Mann, authors of, *Go-Givers Sell More*, for your willingness to allow me to quote from your powerful and inspiring book. I will always remember your gracious and empowering LinkedIn conversation with me. You are heroes to me. Thank you.

Tom Hopkins, author, sales trainer and speaker, and Judy Slack, VP of Development at Tom Hopkins International, for your kindness and generosity when we spoke and for allowing me to share Tom's thoughts about expressing gratitude.

Mike Koenigs, author and speaker for your positive energy, can-do attitude and out-of-the-box thinking. Thank you for allowing me to share an idea from your book, *Money Phone!*.

Ursula Mentjes, my Sales Coach Now Master Mind Coach, for your commitment to helping me succeed, your guidance, generous spirit and wonderful humor.

Rebekah Hall, my other Sales Coach Now Master Mind Coach, for your brilliant business mind, steady support of my efforts and loving nature.

Allison Maslan, Business Coach extraordinaire and founder of the Pinnacle Mastermind, for your insight, support and belief in me. Thank you.

My Pinnacle Mastermind teammates who are supporting and following me on this journey, Haydee Antezana, Liz Papagni, Josh Canova, Gila Kurtz, Don Williams, Pam Hopman, Karen Gwartzman, Heather Harold, Ron Morrow, Grace Moniz and Lisa Thomas.

## Acknowledgements & Gratitude

JuliAnn Stitick, my image consultant for giving me a reason to buy gorgeous clothing and helping me to put my best foot forward and not trip over it. Love you!

Jaime and Steve Geffner, my video production team for your direction, patience and amazing support. You never seem to reach the end of your rope with me. You must have an endless supply of rope.

Sharon Niemi, my dear friend and amazing hairstylist, for your insight, grace, sense of humor and honesty. I love you!

Dan McLaughlin, my high school Speech Team Coach and best teacher I have ever had, for your patience (God help you, when I fell through a hole in the stage during a West Side Story rehearsal.) and your guidance that gave me the foundation and courage to build the sales career I have had.

Mrs. Smock, my eighth grade English teacher who saw something in me that I didn't know I possessed and who is responsible for introducing me to Dan McLaughlin, my high school Speech Team Coach.

Paula and Dan Landess, our dear friends, for your friendship, laughter and support that has gotten me through many of my bad choices and periods of devastation. We love who you are and how you make us feel when we're all together especially, when we reminisce about my Dad and his hairnet. (You had to be there.)

Mary Turilli, my forever ISU Speech Team buddy and college roommate, for your love and support all these years and for the laughter we share each time we have a conversation.

Mary Ann and Corey Lutz, our dear friends, who have been there for us in good times and in the lowest of lows. Thank you for being who you are.

Janice Beighy, owner of Tower Insurance and your team, Lisa, Elsa, Gerardo, Anna, Ralph, Denny and Abby, for your willingness to be a part of the promotion of this book.

Wanda Sebastiano, my Key Accounts Manager, for your determination to have me be a part of your team, patience when you discovered what a handful I am, belief in me to know that I always have the customer's best interests at heart and for being the best example of a salesperson that I have ever seen. You are my mentor but you are also my trusted friend.

Rachel Casavant, my Premise Manager, for your steadiness, patience, foresight and devotion to whatever cause you undertake. You are an inspiration, a force to be reckoned with and my forever friend.

My Nevada City family Helen and Stan Adcock, Dr. Gary Glaze and Teri Dougherty, John and Carolyn Pryor, John, Teri and Jack Mittelstadt for your support, in so many ways.

Nina Sebastiano, for being my cheerleader, loving supporter and Aiden's (my Golden Retriever) loyal companion when we are away. Love you, girl!

Gale Wickham, former Senior VP of Sales, AT&T Advertising Solutions, for your leadership, direction and ability to stay the course even when "White Walkers" were everywhere.

Momma Marcy Royce, for your unwavering love, support and positive spirit that you possess at the age of 98. I love you to pieces!

Carol Royce Wild, for your determination, commitment and friendship.

## Acknowledgements & Gratitude

Raul Rodriguez, founder and owner of Power Pro Plumbing, and one of the most challenging yet, rewarding customers I have ever served. Raul, your demand for quality service made me a better salesperson. Being responsible for your account caused me to hold my company to a higher standard. You raised the bar. Thank you for allowing me to serve you through my products and services and for validating that doing the right thing for the right reason is never wrong.

Throughout my professional sales career, I have worked with amazing people who positively touched my life in a way that made me a better salesperson and I want to thank these colleagues, support staff and managers. Scott Bouchard, Barry Agin, Fuad Burki, Teri Mittelstadt, Marianne Voragen, Mary McEniry, Tim Morrissey, Michelle Clausen, Bob Gray, LeeAnn Sandoval, Rick Holliday, Rachel Casavant, Toni Henderson, Norm Becker, Mary Ann Polson, Kos Semonski, Meredith Montgomery, Liz Paulus, Charmaine Powell, Anthony Torres, Michelle Martinez, Dawn Sullivan-Bell, Piper Godwin, Ron Morgan, Jerry Martinez, Bill Otis, Vi Clark, Barry Matheny, Joyce Sunde, Mike Brock, Michael Autry, Aude Goode, Kathy Wilson, Michele Beach, Jean Knutson, Howard Knutson, Terry Payton, Bill Brewer, Nancy Arteman, Laura Volberding, Barbara Bullard, Otis Lenoir, Mike Hambus, Louie Lobato, John McDonald, Jason Crabtree, Tim Snow, Mike Haake, Denny Payne, Francois Derochers, Shelly Wright, Laura Young, Tony Masese, Kamyar Kashani, Bill Hamilton, Gina Baca, Nancy Arteman Lehman, Karen Boocher, Donna Dyson, Teresa Keenan,

William Silesky, Jodelle Pulda-Ganter, Coby Harral, Rick Mercer, Patricia Bikholz, Tim Snow, Stuart Lachman, Cathy Provost, Rosemary Zarn, Rob Santana, Matt Crowley, Jill Lenmark-Kosciuk, Bill Ingino, David Lawrence, Lou Tielli, Diona Allen, Kim Parra, Elaine Mouw, Matty Moro, Paul Sherman, Ginny Finn, Steve Sanders, Carol Martin, Patricia Thompson, Felicia Keeton, Robert McGee, Dennis Yardley, Lillian Baltes, Bertha Campos, Donny Hudson, Danny Deal, Dan Herrmann, Cherry Dillingham, David Gleason and Marilyn Carlson Neal.

And I want to thank everyone else I have neglected to include. So many have been an inspiration to me. I could not do what I do without your friendship, support and belief in me.

Thank you.

# Acknowledgements & Gratitude

Don't Sell. Let Them Buy.™

## About the Author

Bestselling Author, Award-Winning Sales Executive, Sales Coach, and Speaker, Chiqeeta Jameson has more than 30 years of sales experience working for major corporations in telephone sales, outside sales and national sales training. She is also the founder and lead coaching consultant at Chiqeeta V. Jameson, Inc.

Working as one of over 5000 sales representatives at a major telecommunications corporation, Chiqeeta rose to become the company's top-selling online advertising sales representative for five consecutive years by generating over 6M in revenue. This success led upper management to commission her to create a training video for other sales representatives and new hires in her approach to her sales call.

## About the Author

Chiqeeta is also a breast cancer survivor and advocate for educating women about breast-density—especially about dense-breast tissue and the care that is needed beyond mammography. This advocacy work led her to accept a position as Director of Sales and subsequently, Director of Marketing and Women's Health Advocacy for a medical manufacturing company.

Today, Chiqeeta specializes in helping sales teams, entrepreneurs and sales professionals who have lost their way or have a broken sales career. She also trains those new to sales, in how to develop a solid sales conversation structure and skill set through the teaching of her 9-Step Don't Sell. Let Them Buy™, Sales Conversation Process.

Chiqeeta's ability to blend humor and skill-building strategies makes her a desired motivational speaker. An engaging, knowledgeable storyteller, Chiqeeta has an uncanny ability to take her audience on a journey that not only teaches but uplifts and challenges them to excel personally and professionally.

Chiqeeta holds a Bachelor of Science degree in Speech Communication Education from Illinois State University where she was awarded a four-year scholarship and excelled as a winning member of the ISU Forensics Team. She is a member of the National Association of Women Business Owners, the E Women Network and serves on the Women in Business Committee, Culver City Chamber of Commerce. She is also a frequent speaker at women's events and has been a speaker on the TEDx stage at Loyola Marymount University, Los Angeles, California.

Chiqeeta lives in Los Angeles with her husband Craig Jameson, an architect specializing in the design of independent schools, along with Aiden McCormack the Jameson, their Golden Retriever.

**To learn more about working with Chiqeeta, accessing her online programs, or to book Chiqeeta to speak at your event, please visit www.ChiqeetaJameson.com or email cj@chiqeetajameson.com.**

Don't Sell. Let Them Buy.™

www.ingramcontent.com/pod-product-compliance
Lightning Source LLC
Chambersburg PA
CBHW020636220526
45464CB00001B/167